Clauspeter Becker/Jürgen Lewandowski

HONDA
Portrait of an International Brand

With contributions from

Herbert Völker
Heinz Prüller
Günther Molter

Delius Klasing Verlag

Die deutsche Bibliothek – CIP-Einheitsaufnahme

HONDA: Portrait of an International Brand/Clauspeter Becker/Jürgen Lewandowski.
With contributions from Herbert Völker ... [Publ. HONDA Deutschland GmbH,
Public Relations and Press Department. English translations: Colin Brazier].
– 1st edition – Bielefeld: Delius Klasing, 2000
ISBN 3-7688-1100-X

The brand logo is reproduced by kind permission of HONDA Deutschland GmbH,
Offenbach

Publisher: HONDA Deutschland GmbH, Public Relations and Press
Department, Willy Cohnen

1st edition
ISBN 3-7688-1100-X
Copyright by Verlag Delius, Klasing & Co. KG, Bielefeld

Editorial assistance: Monika Lewandowski
English translations: Colin Brazier, Munich
Layout: Ekkehard Schonart
Jacket design: Gabriele Engel
Photos: HONDA company archives
except for pages 188, 191 (3), 194 (2) and 195 (2): Günther Molter;
pages 60, 68, 69, 70, 71, 80, 82, 94, 95, 98, 108, 112 (top),
113, 160 and 161: Peter Vann
Blockmaking: Service vor dem Druck, Bielefeld
Printing: Kunst- und Werbedruck, Bad Oeynhausen
Printed in Germany 2000

Delius Klasing Verlag, Siekerwall 21, D-33602 Bielefeld
Tel. (+49) 521-559-0; Fax (+49) 521-559-113
e-mail: info@delius-klasing.de
http://www.delius-klasing.de

CONTENTS

SUCCESS IS THE RESULT OF
INSPIRATION AND LABOR

Soichiro Honda

SOICHIRO HONDA

A MAN
AND HIS
DREAMS

Nobody would dispute Soichiro Honda's gift of being able to arrive on the scene at the right time with the right idea. Nevertheless, his bold self-confidence and individuality, so difficult for the Japanese to understand (combined with the fact that he questioned many Japanese dogmas) turned him into an outsider, with views and insights that were difficult to communicate.

A MAN AND HIS DREAMS

Soichiro Honda had a brilliant but stubborn mind. As his memoirs confirm, he had a spontaneous tendency to defend the decisions he made with a tenacity all his own.

In the early 1970s, for instance, this selfsame tendency caused Soichiro Honda to drive his own company practically to the brink of ruin. Contrary to the advice of his engineers, he clung to the concept of air-cooled passenger car engines, which were no longer able to comply with increasingly strict US emission laws. It fell to his business partner and the co-founder of the company, Takeo Fujisawa, to prevent the impending disaster with an ultimatum, the like of which Japanese industry had never seen before. Fujisawa confronted Honda with an alternative: he could remain President of the Honda Motor Company Ltd. and choose not to realize his policies, or he could step down, rejoin the ranks of lower-level engineers, and continue to work on perfecting his ideas.

In Honda's memoirs we read the following about this decisive phase: "I had to decide quickly. Fujisawa's statement upset me greatly, but I began to realize where my obstinacy had taken me. My answer was clear: I wanted to remain President. But that also meant that, without any reservations, I had to allow our engineers to work on the water-cooling system that I had stubbornly refused to countenance for three years."

Here we see another side of the man: Once he made a decision, he stood behind it one hundred percent — even if it ran counter to his previous plans and ideas. And he bore no grudge against those who, difficult though it sometimes was, had persuaded him to change course.

Soichiro Honda was born on November 17, 1906 in the village of Komyo in the Prefecture of Shizuoka. He was the first of nine children born to the village blacksmith. His mother not only cared for the growing family but also for the three or four apprentices that Soichiro's father, Gihei Honda, was always training in his blacksmith's shop.

As a youngster, Honda (if we can believe his memoirs) was a lively, wide-awake child who mainly attracted attention with his pranks, indulged in all kinds of nonsense with his friends and enjoyed a remarkably pleasant childhood. We all know that older gentlemen tend to glorify the days of their youth and the past — yet it does seem that Soichiro Honda enjoyed a degree of freedom that was unusual in the Japan of those days. And he seems to have come from an exceptional home that allowed him more independence than was customary at the time. Honda comments on this subject: "The country was too poor to think about setting up a 'kindergarten'. So I enjoyed a lot of freedom at home until I was six years old. My parents were busy: my father in his smithy, my mother running the

A MAN AND HIS DREAMS

One of the earliest pictures we have of Soichiro Honda (l.) shows him in school uniform with a friend, while attending the village school near Hamamatsu

household and visiting neighboring families. Only my grandfather kept an eye on me from a distance – from a considerable distance. Father and Mother devoted very little attention to my education. They never forced me to read a book if I didn't want to. In our remote area, far from the cities and from progress, life was still governed strongly by old traditions.

"Until they started school, the children were the kings of the home – and were allowed to get away with everything. In this way, their characters were formed: Each child complied with his or her temperament, sensed approval, and became accustomed to taking responsibility for his or her own actions. In the end, that was better than ordering the children around and punishing them. Later came school, with its very tough rules and strict discipline. But thanks to the freedom I had enjoyed, I was better prepared to grow accustomed to the hard realities of life, to the need for integration into an existing order, and to the resulting social pressures."

It certainly seems that Soichiro Honda enjoyed more freedom than the other children with whom he played. The number of complaints from the neighbors and his reputation of being the initiator of many a prank must have caused considerable discomfiture to his parents, who had a sense of morals and order. In his memoirs, Honda again and again refers to the influence of his father: "He limited himself to teaching me just a few principles,

ones that I have always followed: Always keep your word, never lie, and maintain a worthy stance. Morality is really a simple matter – it is based on reason and good judgement. Nevertheless, as soon as other people were involved, my father became very strict. If I had been dishonest, lied to someone, or said wicked things about the neighbors, I got a slap and a lecture, which was doubly hard for me to take. Yet looking back, I'm thankful for his strictness."

If there was a moment in Soichiro Honda's life that proved decisive in the years that followed, it was probably an incident that took place while he was still very young: "I was two or three years old, and not yet able to tell the seasons apart. Was it winter, spring or summer? We lived in a village that had not yet been overtaken by the latest technologies. But in the fields near our house I heard an engine – and I knew right away that this noise, which sounded like music in my ears, would accompany me for the rest of my life. It was the rice dehusking machine on a farm about a mile and a quarter away. From the veranda of our wooden house I could see the bluish trail of smoke issuing from the machine. One day I asked my grandfather to give me a ride there – and this soon became a habit. In rain or sunshine, I had to get to that machine, which emitted a series of infernal banging and hissing noises; I had to see it, smell it and hear it."

A MAN AND HIS DREAMS

The die had obviously been cast. Soichiro Honda had found his calling. And with all the determination for which he is known, he began to organize his life accordingly. "I did what I could to sit out of sight of my teachers, so that I could daydream or sleep when I wanted. I discovered that there were several dangerous seats: near the blackboard (where the teacher usually stood to explain something), in the last row (where the teacher often walked round to check up on what we were doing) and at the window seats (to which daydreamers and lazy kids were supposed to feel drawn). I didn't care must for these seats, since the clouds and sky offered me hardly any inspiration for my secret machine plans. In the middle of the class, surrounded by a small bunch of diligent classmates, I felt less exposed to the teacher's view. Unfortunately, it was the grades that determined where each pupil sat. The worst of them were put in the front row, directly under the strict teacher's gaze, whereas the best ones had more freedom in the back rows. I had to ensure that my grades were good enough to allow me to keep my seat in the middle. To do this I relied on mathematics, drawing, and singing. These were the only subjects I was good at, but they made up for my complete incompetence in the others. In this way I skilfully concealed myself among the masses and was able to continue reflecting on my little inventions."

When Soichiro was eight years old he caught sight of an automobile for the first time. That first car must have been a Ford. The chauffeur watched over it "like a temple keeper". One day, a large poster was put up announcing the appearance of an American pilot on the parade ground of the nearby city of Hamamatsu: "By that time, I had become an airplane specialist, and a leading designer of peculiar miniature airplanes made out of bamboo rods and driven by elastic bands. Now I wanted to find out to what extent my models corresponded with reality. On a billboard I read that a charge would be made to see the show. I worked out the entrance fee: it seemed like a lot of money to me. In the event, I managed to help myself to the entire sum from my father's wallet."

After a strenuous bicycle ride to Hamamatsu, which was nearly 16 miles away, the young Honda experienced the exciting show put on by American pilot Niles Smith. After the 16-mile trip home, he arrived there tired and beat. Nor can the reception he received have been exactly full of enthusiasm. It is easy to imagine the scene:. On the one side was Father, worried and also hopping mad; on the other side, an enthusiastic Soichiro, full of dreams and plans, and still captivated by his first encounter with an airplane. The enthusiasm must have been contagious: Soichiro told his father all about the new inventions and explained things to him that the village blacksmith had never heard of.

A MAN AND HIS DREAMS

The father had the boy explain the shape of the airplane, the propeller, and the controls in the cockpit. His son's enthusiasm for the new technology seems to have ignited his own interest. He wanted to know if the boy had sat in the airplane, or even had a chance to fly in it. The boy's response provides ample evidence of pragmatism: "If somebody had invited me to climb aboard, I would probably have refused. After all, if an airplane crashes, you die for sure. There's nothing you can do about it." He wanted to spare his parents any such misery.

Technology had grabbed him. Honda later told the American journalist Sol Sanders: "The first car I ever encountered was losing oil as it went past. In the truest sense of the word, I was enchanted by the smell of that oil. I leaned over the spot of oil, put my nose up to it, and rubbed my hands in the residue. From that moment on I knew that I would make cars some day."

But first he had to get through school. After completing Yanahigashi Primary School he moved on to Futamata Senior Primary School in 1919, which he left in 1922 with respectable grades. School was never much fun for Soichiro Honda: besides his strong preference for only a few subjects (balanced by corresponding weaknesses in the others) and the grades that resulted from this, he also seemed to have problems holding his own among the other kids of his age. On the one hand, this was due to the fact that he had to help out a lot in his father's smithy, which led to him acquiring something of a reputation as a dirty slob. On the other hand, his mother tended to dress him up in particularly bright colors for holiday celebrations. It is no wonder that the other kids picked on young Soichiro whenever they could.

Later he reacted in his own way: He took no notice of all the talk, but wore particularly ostentatious clothing: red and pink became his favorite colors, which he wore as often as possible. Non-conformity was now the principle on which he based his life, and in this way he tried to set himself apart from the behavior of the average man in the street. This led him to discover that artists and inventors should not conform, and that they were even obligated to the pursuit of non-conformity.

In 1917 or 1918 his father opened up a bicycle store and workshop. For this business he subscribed to a magazine entitled The World of Wheels, which Soichiro read with great enthusiasm. His desire to work with engines grew from day to day and his enthusiasm increased with every article, every technical description, and every photograph: "I really only had one fixed idea, and that was to be involved with engines, to invent machines, and to get real greasy with machine oil and lubricant."

A MAN AND HIS DREAMS

Soichiro was just 15 years old when he saw a small ad in The World of Wheels, in which a repair shop for bicycles and motorcycles made its services public. The name of the workshop made him curious: "Shokai Workshops, Company for Automotive Technology in Tokyo." Honda wrote them a letter of application and was immediately offered an apprenticeship. The offer also convinced his father. His son, who could not be persuaded to stay at school, was allowed to take the risk of moving to Tokyo. For Soichiro, the offer must have seemed like a great deliverance: "I don't think I even looked back as I crossed the threshold of my parents house and traveled to Tokyo."

His father brought him to that distant city, to the fascinating metropolis of an Empire. The two of them must have been overcome with astonishment — they had never before been farther than the provincial city of Hamamatsu: "We were amazed again and again by the great wealth and superabundance to be seen everywhere in Tokyo."

Soichiro Honda spent six years in Tokyo, a period during which he learned much and earned such a good reputation that, despite his youth, the Shokai Workshops would send him out to visit the customers. Many of them didn't take the young man seriously at first, but were later so satisfied with his work that they sent letters of thanks to his company's boss.

The fifteen-year-old was confronted with his first great challenge after just a few months; a devastating earthquake turned Tokyo into a heap of rubble on September 1, 1922. The death toll of over 70,000 still gives us an impression today of the forces of nature that were unleashed on that day. "A far-off grumbling came from the depths of the earth. The ground began to shake. The buildings groaned on their foundations as though crowbars where prying at their roots. Walls of flame shot up everywhere. It was hardly possible to walk because the earth, now torn open, was shaken by violent jolts similar to the burping of some giant drunkard. The earth acted crazy, spewed fire, shook in all its cracks and flung huge masses of water into the air that carried away everything on the shore in a powerful flood."

The master of the workshop knew what the most precious possession in his collapsible building was: the automobiles. He called out to his apprentices: "Save the cars!" Everyone jumped into a car as fast as he could — for Honda, it was a strange situation in which to be learning to drive a car. "I could not believe my eyes: between the burning houses, the screaming crowd, and the ground moving in all directions underneath my feet, I was to sit behind the wheel of a car for the first time. I had a good deal of difficulty putting the car into gear and driving it down the road. I drove very slowly so that I did not run over the people rushing out of the houses, and

kept moving until I reached an open space outside the city where I thought I was safe from the fire. I had won! I had saved my life, saved a car from destruction, and in the process driven one for the first time."

It is not surprising that Soichiro earned a high reputation so quickly despite his youth: he had strong nerves, was constantly improving his skills, could take a lot of hard treatment, and always stayed curious. During these six years Honda remained faithful to Mr. Sakakibara and his Shokai Company. He learned everything worth knowing back then about building, repairing, and driving cars, and the multitude of different brands that were brought in for repair gave him a broad base of experience.

In 1928, when he was 22 years old, the young man was offered the chance of opening a branch of the Shokai Workshops in Hamamatsu. And so he returned proudly home and had a big sign put up: "Shokai Workshops – Hamamatsu Branch." "I was finally a real man: independent and in full command of my own arms and legs, my brain, my fate, and my time – and also the risk, from which I was determined not to shy away."

The new branch was not without its rivals, but Honda developed a method which he felt could not possibly fail: In order to win over new customers and to prove to competitors that he was the undisputed best, he made it his task to tackle difficult jobs that the competitors would not risk taking on. And his repairs had to be faster too, so that cus-

From 1928 on, this building was the starting point of Soichiro Honda's remarkable career: the Art Automobile Service Station gained an excellent reputation within a very short time

A MAN AND HIS DREAMS

tomers who did not want to be without their car for very long would also come to him.

He plunged into his work in this spirit, and worked at night and at the weekends as well. Soon he had built up the good reputation that made him a leading local businessman. And the financial side also went well – even as a young man, Honda earned excellent money. This made some of the prominent people of the town jealous. "I was one of the few industrialists in town to own my own car. The 'old money' was outraged that I had secured such a top spot in the establishment as a young man. In Japan, age is very important. The young are not regarded as credible. You have to reach a certain age if you do not want to be considered an adventurer."

Soichiro Honda's penchant for inventing things was already in full swing. During the fire that had followed the big earthquake back in Tokyo, he saw that the wooden spokes normally used on cars back then quickly caught fire. So he made the decision – largely based on the experience he had gained in the parental blacksmith's shop – to begin producing steel wheels. "I patented this invention – which seems primitive now but was a real revolution back then. I was thirty years old. My steel rims were very successful. People liked them because they were rigid and practical. Soon they were being exported, particularly to India, where cars had

to travel long distances on poor roads." But Honda was not satisfied with these successes. He wanted to become more famous and to fulfil his childhood dream of designing and building cars that would bear his own name. Honda had already had an initial taste of the adventure of leading his own company, which he later described as follows: "Managing a workshop is like driving a bus or a small country train. They stop in every village and take all the people with them, but they are never used for long distances. It is certainly possible to be happy with a small train line, but I was more ambitious and wanted to drive larger trains at higher speeds."

Once again, it was an insight gained from everyday life that was to change Honda's future. Just as the all too easily combustible wooden spokes had led to steel wheels, examination of his company's repair department brought him the next idea: There was a constant lack of piston rings, and many repairs could not be finished because the rings (which weight for weight were more expensive than pure silver) were not available for delivery. These parts did not require much in the way of raw materials, so material procurement, storage, and financing did not present a problem. So together with a few partners – including his father – Honda founded a new company, Tokai Seiki, for the manufacture of piston rings.

A MAN AND HIS DREAMS

Nevertheless: "A good idea alone is not enough. I had difficulty making the molds for the piston rings, and then pouring the rings out of steel or a similar material. The first products proved unfit for sale. Our piston rings were hard as a rock, and therefore not resilient enough for an engine. I would have liked to learned the secret of a more elastic material from the foundrymen in our area, but they refused to speak to me about it and entrust a stranger with their processes."

In this situation, Honda once again proved his tenacity. For months he toiled away every night in his laboratory, performing a series of experiments. He mixed alloys and tried new melting methods, but each time the results were disappointing: the piston rings were unusable, and they stayed that way. Eventually, the strain caused by his daily work at the company and the night shifts in the laboratory was too much – the doctors prescribed a two-month stay at a health resort.

Once he returned to work, Soichiro Honda realized that while he had outstanding practical experience, his knowledge of basic theory was pretty deficient. With typical determination, he turned to the Hamamatsu Institute of Technology and approached the professors there. After listening to his description of the problem, they confirmed right away that his alloy was lacking in silicon. "Since I did not even know that there was

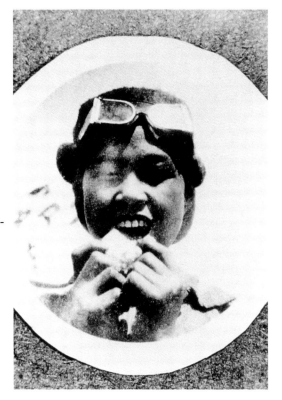

This young student became a successful businessman who was able to indulge his hobby of motor racing and win various trophies. After a serious accident in 1936, Honda put an end to this aspect of his career

As a student, Soichiro Honda must have made quite an impression in Hamamatsu. His professors made their way to the Institute on bicycles or on foot, but Honda, the former racing car driver (he resigned from car racing in 1936 after a fearsome accident in the All-Japan Speed Rally, but not before he had set up a new Japanese speed record) roared onto campus in his own car. While his fellow students had freshly washed shirts and clean fingernails, took careful lecture notes, and later memorized what they had written, Honda often came to the lecture hall directly from the factory with greasy hands and a dirty collar, and was satisfied with trying to put what he had learned into practice with the aid of a sketch or a simple calculation.

In short: his behavior led to jealousy and suspicion among his professors and fellow students. Honda naturally regarded this as further confirmation of his deep contempt for everything that was school-like and pedantic: "The students' attitude surprised me. They didn't really try to understand anything. Instead, they just took their notes and learned all the theories by heart without drawing any conclusions or verifying the theories with the aid of experiments."

The biggest annoyance was caused by the examinations, for which Honda refused on principle to sit: "Why should I have continued to deal with the same questions and return to things that I have long since under-

such a thing as silicon, I was bitterly disappointed." So Honda made a quick decision to matriculate at the Institute of Technology – a somewhat rash choice, since he should have known right from the start that his strong, individualistic character would be confronted with massive opposition from the rigid university system. At first, the division of labor worked. In the morning, the young entrepreneur listened politely to the lectures in Hamamatsu, and in the evening tried to put what he had learned into practice. In between he also had to take care of his company, to which he felt obligated by his strong sense of honor. "My friends – and above all my father – had counted on me, and so had all those who worked with me. I did not have the right to disappoint these people, but on the other hand, I had to study at the Institute in order to be able to draw up technical plans, and to implement my theoretical ideas as a real engineer."

Soichiro Honda among his employees at the Art Shokai company's branch in Hamamatsu, which he opened in his home town in 1928, when he was 22

A MAN AND HIS DREAMS

stood and already done in practice? The only thing that interested me was acquiring the knowledge I lacked as quickly as possible. I was so irritated by the cumbersome, awkward nature of the university system, that I only went to lectures that dealt with practical problems related to piston rings. I admit that I ignored the university regulations, but after all, I was the first student to decide for himself what he wanted to learn."

This period of suffering – student by day, inventor by night, and head of a blossoming company in between – lasted barely two years. The inevitable then happened: Mr. Adashi, Director of the Institute of Technology, informed his unusual alumnus that he had been removed from the register of students. Later, Soichiro Honda was able to reconstruct the dialog that followed: 'What am I being accused of?' I asked. 'You refuse to take the exams, and without these results, you will never get your degree,' responded the director. 'I know that – but what difference does it make?' was my answer. 'If you don't get a degree, then I can't see what benefit your education here is supposed to have!' Honda failed to convince the director that he did not want a degree at all, but only to gain knowledge for practical applications. 'A degree,' I told the Director, 'is worth less than a ticket to a movie. With a movie ticket you can at least enter the cinema and enjoy a

pleasant evening – but a degree doesn't ensure you entry into life.'
None of this helped in the least: Soichiro Honda had to leave the Institute of Technology. After that, he began studying technical literature with a private teacher. Director Adashi, incidentally, later regretted his decision, as Honda remembers with a clear sense of satisfaction: "In a telephone call, he confirmed to me that I was his biggest educational error."

In order to understand the later dynamism of Soichiro Honda's life and companies, it is important to know all these facts. They explain his deep mistrust of universities, his disliking of the well-trodden path, and the decisions he so often made to put capable people in high positions even while they were still young. The experience that he gained with his fellow students in Hamamatsu strengthened his conviction that students with the best average grades were not always the most intelligent or skilled, and therefore not the most promising members of their clan. He was firmly convinced that they were simply the ones who were best able to adapt to the system, do the best theoretical work, and get the best grades in tests covering a limited range of topics: "A degree is a piece of paper that confirms that, during his or her youth, the student was diligent, disciplined, and probably quite detached from real life."

A MAN AND HIS DREAMS

Despite all this, the Hamamatsu Institute of Technology was one of the crucial elements in Honda's later life, since he was finally able, with the aid of his professors, to manufacture piston rings that possessed the required properties after all. There were considerable weaknesses in the initial series, but a start had been made; and after many a night spent burning the candle at both ends, the dimensions and the tolerances also complied with the required standards. Honda had won. The new company's products sold extremely well, and it soon became necessary to build a new factory in Awata, in the Prefecture of Shizuoka.

Piston rings for passenger car engines were soon joined by rings and engine blocks for airplanes and ships – no wonder that one of the country's industrial giants, the Toyota corporation, suggested cooperation and fusion. Since Toyota had become Honda's main customer for piston rings, the planned merger seemed a logical step. Nevertheless, Japan's entry into World War II prevented it. Honda concentrated on automating the production in his factories, since more and more workers were being sent off to the front. In this way, he became familiar with the basic principles of assembly line working.

The qualities of this self-made-man had by then become widely known, and came to the notice of the government in Tokyo. Honda was asked one day to give some thought to the production of airplane propellers, which back then required about a week's production time, since the skills involved were complex and time-consuming. "I invented a system that made it possible to produce two propellers automatically in precisely thirty minutes. I was inspired above all by the French designer Lathier, whose patents, however, I was unable to see, since France – as an enemy power – would not reveal them. At least we were able to save the patent fees."

With achievements of this kind, it was no wonder that Honda quickly became something of a national hero, quoted as a role model for many companies. He remained, however, critical of himself: "When I compared my propellers with the French ones after the war, I had to admit that mine were inferior."

For Honda, as for many Japanese, the capitulation in 1945 was a shock: "For me, the fact that the American airplanes were able to shoot down ours, which we thought were the best designs in the world, was a sign that we would lose the war." The Honda factories were destroyed by American bombs. After the war, he shared the same fear as many of his countrymen: "Now the foreigners will come and set themselves up in Japan."

A MAN AND HIS DREAMS

Soichiro Honda drew different conclusions from this than most of his countrymen: "Let them come – there are still so many areas in which we can show them the performance we're capable of!" Soichiro Honda was prepared to seek out and find these areas.

The Tenno's surrender greatly humbled Japan. The Japanese islands, which had remained unconquered for more than a thousand years, were occupied by the Americans – Japan had not only lost a war, but lost face as well. At first, Soichiro Honda fled to another world: "For a year I did little else but play the shakuhachi (an old instrument similar to a flute) and the koto (a type of harp). Despite the circumstances, I was happy and had time to think about my future." He bought a still, brewed rice wine, and drank it with friends and neighbors, a situation that seriously disquieted his wife, who hardly recognised her once so industrious and successful husband. Nevertheless, he did not stay completely inactive for long. He drove around the country a lot and tried to grasp the general mood. He wanted to do business again, but was not sure where to seek his chance.

Engineers and inventors had a rough time in the Japan of 1945. The US, as the occupying power, had not yet determined a clear course for Japan – some politicians spoke in favor of a method similar to the Morgenthau Plan (which the politician of the same name wanted to use in Germany). This plan would have turned Japan back into an agricultural country. Industry was not to be encouraged, and therefore engines for cars, ships, and airplanes would no longer be in demand.

With a motorcycle saved from the ravages of war, Honda traveled around the devastated country; his car, which he still owned, had to be taken off the road because there was not enough fuel available. During these tours, Honda discovered a new magic word: mobility. Almost everyone to whom Honda spoke had a relative whom he wanted to visit in order to exchange goods and get food. With the railroad network severely damaged, and the few buses that were still intact making only slow progress on the miserable roads (not to mention strict fuel rationing that restricted even those who did own motorcycles or cars), the bicycle became the most favored means of transportation, the beast of burden, and the family coach –a jack of all trades.

Soichiro Honda had discovered his market, but since he did not want to plunge into an adventure, he remained cautious. Instead, he advanced in small steps: In October 1946, he founded the Honda Technical Research Institute. The land upon which the pre-war factories had once stood before being destroyed by American bombs, was of course still there, but the bombers had done their work thoroughly, and the only place left for his first lab-

A MAN AND HIS DREAMS

oratory was a shack 24 square meters (258 square feet) in size. The fresh start was anything but rosy, but Honda did have some start-up capital, acquired through the sale of his Tokai Seiki piston ring factory (or what was left of it) to Toyota.

It is understandable that Honda's first idea was to build engines – and he was lucky. In a military warehouse formerly occupied by the Imperial Army, he discovered 500 gasoline-powered engines that had been used to drive generators for radio equipment. As we have seen, fuel rationing in Japan was a major problem at the time. To make matters worse, bicycles with auxiliary engines (Honda quickly figured out how to add a limited amount of vitality to a bicycle by attaching a two-cycle engine) led to envy and resentment among those who did not own one. Before long he was accused of acting unpatriotically, since these vehicles were useless in the light of the scarcity of fuel, and therefore only made profits easier to come by for dealers on the black market. Hardly anyone listened to his arguments that the machines had minimal fuel consumption levels and would also make it easier for people to travel out into the countryside to collect their food supplies.

Once again the young factory owner's improvisational skills were needed. He found the desired patriotic solution: Together with his father, Honda purchased a spruce forest.

From the roots of the fallen trees he extracted an oil resembling turpentine and used it to stretch gasoline, which he usually purchased on the black market. The solution had occurred to him when he remembered that, in the final years of the war, the Japanese air force had flown its missions on a mixture of pine resin and gasoline. Although he did not regard the mixture as entirely convincing – "I don't know if I would have felt safe in a resin-powered airplane" – the risk of falling out of the sky did not seem all that high for his mopeds.

The Yamashita factory was where, in 1946, Soichiro Honda started his breathtaking career as a manufacturer of auxiliary bicycle engines and motorcycles

With such basic vehicles as this bicycle with auxiliary engine, Japan struggled to get mobile again after the Second World War

Soichiro Honda and Takeo Fujisawa (r) directed the company from 1949 on

Soichiro Honda's business with motorcycles and motor scooters grew – and he was proud of his products

The young entrepreneur's elan also had a negative side: "One day I wanted to improve the resin yield, so I decided to use a small charge of dynamite in order to blow open the bark of the tree and collect the resin. Unfortunately the dynamite exploded too early, and within a few minutes my forest was reduced to a heap of ashes."

Notwithstanding this setback, Honda knew what to do: He simply purchased spruce trees from other forest owners.

He had no trouble with financing. His 500 modified ex-army engines were sold in a jiffy; demand was so great that people lined up in the street to buy them. Simultaneously with the production of his power-assisted bicycles, Honda had begun designing his own engine.

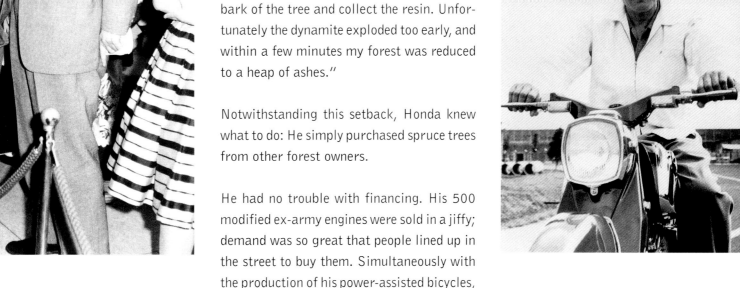

This power brew was by no means perfect – eye-witnesses reported that the engines needed up to fifteen minutes of intensive pedaling before they hesitantly agreed to start, and the black clouds of exhaust that trailed behind the bikes led to the engine being given the nickname of the 'chimney'. But in due course the police authorities and various other envious people had to admit: it really did save fuel. When checks were made it was usually enough to ask the examiners to sniff at the exhaust pipe – "You can smell that I'm running on turpentine!" – and the riders were allowed to pass.

Honda was back in action. The gifted engineer recognized that his country, which slowly began to recover from the ravages of war, had a huge pent-up demand for transportation. He also recognized that the future would not belong to the maker of an auxiliary engine for bicycles, but to the maker of a real motorcycle power unit – or better still to the manufacturer of complete motorcycles. He linked this knowledge with a guiding principle (which the company has not changed to this day): "First man, then machine." His products were required to orient themselves to the desires of potential users – a guiding principle that was followed consistently and

A MAN AND HIS DREAMS

enabled the company to ensure that, in the decades to come, it never produced products unwanted by the market.

As always, Honda took resolute action: First he recruited Kiyoshi Kawashima, a young engineer who had just completed his studies at the Hamamatsu Institute of Technology. The choice seems to have been a good one, since Kawashima become one of the company's pioneers in the decades that followed. From 1973 to 1983, he was even president of the company.

As Kawashima set about developing the Type A, the company's first real motorcycle, along with its engine, Honda had one idea after another: How about a larger, bored-out engine that would be strong enough to power a tricycle-like vehicle with a load platform? Weren't there many small-business owners who would buy such a vehicle? In due course, this vehicle (named the Type B) also became a hit. As early as October 1948, Honda had a 66 percent share of the domestic market. No wonder this successful businessman was then able to liquidate his Technical Research Institute and found the Honda Motor Company, Ltd. with an initial capital of one million yen (back then, about 5,000 dollars).

With the same speed that Honda started up the operation, financial troubles set in. Many of his customers, usually small bicycle shops, went bankrupt in the aftermath of the first post-war recession. Those that were not broke could only pay sporadically. Another stroke of luck made it possible to survive this critical situation as well. In August 1949, Soichiro Honda met and took a liking to Takeo Fujisawa. Just two months later, this young businessman began his career at Honda – a career that would make him the second most important person in the company, after Honda himself, right up until the two left it together in 1973.

Fujisawa was the brilliant businessman at Honda's side. Soichiro Honda always had the highest praise for his partner: "Had I been obliged to manage my company alone, I would have been ruined very quickly. But my friend Fujisawa was there. I owe it to him that the company developed in the way it did." Fujisawa also initiated the first export campaigns. In October 1952, the company delivered its first "Dream" motorcycles to the Philippines, and in November of the same year, Soichiro Honda took his first informative trip to the USA. There he visited many industrial companies, studied their production methods, and bought a large number of machines for use in his factories.

It was these early trips to foreign countries that revealed another facet of Soichiro Honda's personality. During these trips he recognized – long before his Japanese col-

Soichiro Honda remained interested in technical matters all his life – and liked to be with young people

leagues – that the market of the future would be a global one. "Think global, act local" was to become one of his principles, which (beginning in the 1960s) he was to implement throughout the world with a consistency all his own. Incidentally, it was a principle that he linked directly to his guiding motto: "First man, then machine": after all, where was it possible to determine people's desires and longings better than directly where they lived and worked?

The first big trip around the world taught him a second lesson as well: "Motor sport is a good thing – good for the engineers and good for the company image." In March 1954, the company entered the racing game. The first race in which Honda participated was held in Brazil. In June 1954, Honda was a spectator at the legendary Tourist Trophy race on the Isle of Man, and then visited several European factories. After returning home, he gave the order to start developing racing bikes with which the company would compete for the World Motorcycle Championship, and of course, for the Tourist Trophy. The first result was the official Honda works team, with which the company initially competed in the Japanese Motorcycle Championships, starting in November 1955. This laid the cornerstone for one of the great motor sport stories of the post-war period, leading to innumerable World and National Championships on two and four wheels.

Honda, however, faced his biggest challenge in 1962. Towards the end of the 1950s and in the early 1960s, he had reverted to the idea of building his own automobiles: "I believed that every product from the Honda company ought to have an engine and be based on

A MAN AND HIS DREAMS

mechanical engineering principles. I began my life with a passion for engines. I owed them my success, and I wanted to remain true to them."

The decision was made: In the Spring of 1962, Honda made the official announcement that automobile design work was about to begin. Just a few months later, the T 360 and S 360 were presented. This remarkable haste was due to political circumstances. During the course of 1962, the Japanese Government had decided to pass a law that allowed only three companies the right to build automobiles. Prime Minister Ikeda's thinking was evidently as follows: "The more that production is expanded, the more suppliers battling on the market, the lower the price of the products would be, but the competitive battle among too many designers would render the efforts of each individual unprofitable." In plain terms, this meant that the Japanese Government wanted to line up just three companies on their own market. The big role model for this was the United States, where there were also only three major corporations active in this area (General Motors, Ford, and Chrysler).

Honda, as a businessman, first attempted to influence the opinion of government representatives with a press campaign. Why, he asked in advertisements and round-table discussions, should he – as someone who had built up his own company, earned money, and paid an abundance of taxes – not have the right to offer his customers automobiles? In a democratic country, the consumer should decide what he wants, Honda insisted.

The mighty Ministry for Commerce and Industry was not at all impressed by his arguments at first: Ikeda had Parliament vote on the law. Evidently some of the representatives agreed with Honda's arguments' for it was rejected. But the Prime Minister did not let up. He now planned to realize his idea for an organized Japanese automotive industry by issuing directives and enacting regulations, selecting January 1, 1963 as the date on which his reforms would go into effect.

Honda reacted to this affront with a public announcement that he was more determined than ever to begin building automobiles. In order to undermine the government's tactics, the T 360 and S 360 models were shown at diverse exhibitions during October. The danger, however, had not yet passed: These were only the first prototypes, and series production or delivery to customers was inconceivable before mid-1963. Once again Takeo Fujisawa came up with a brilliant idea: The Honda company announced a large-scale competition, in which the public was challenged to guess the price of the new vehicle. The result was overwhelming: Nearly six million responses flooded into Honda headquarters – six million Japanese had taken note of the cars, given them some thought, and

In the years and decades to follow, Honda – as is described in the next chapters – developed into one of the world's most successful automobile and motorcycle companies. The brand was among the first to establish its own production facilities on other continents, as a means of satisfying local customers' needs. It was also the first brand to export cars and motorcycles produced in the USA back to Japan. Later, models were to be introduced that had been designed and built for use only in specific parts of the world.

Behind all this success of course, remained the ideas of Soichiro Honda, who naturally continued to monitor the progress of his company attentively and guide it discreetly (as chairman of the Advisory Board) even after his departure in 1973. He was thus also able to experience the series of triumphs in Formula 1 and the introduction of the Honda NSX, the world's first aluminum car.

For him, the greatest satisfaction probably came when he was enrolled in the Automotive Hall of Fame in Detroit in 1989. There, his life's work is featured alongside such personalities as Gottlieb Daimler, Karl Benz, and Henry Ford. It was a remarkable conclusion to an unusual life, which had begun as the son of a blacksmith in the village of Komyo in the Prefecture of Shizuoka. Soichiro Honda, the man who founded the Honda Motor Co. in 1948 and shaped it, died in August 1991 at the age of 84.

A great moment: In October 1989 Soichiro Honda was elected to the Automotive Hall of Fame in Detroit; this was the last foreign visit which the 82-year-old Honda, seen here with his wife, was to undertake

assigned them a price. Honda speculated very accurately that these six million would also be prepared to support a vociferous protest if the government were to forbid Honda to build and deliver the vehicles. But things never got that far, and all attempts to limit the number of Japanese car manufacturers to three failed. Early in 1964, the government gave up its plans, and the way was clear. Once again, Soichiro Honda had achieved his aims through persistence and resourcefulness – simultaneously highlighting to perfection his reputation as an atypical Japanese who was not willing to accept official dictates.

THE RISE TO THE TOP BEGINS

THOUGH IT WAS NOT UNTIL 1948 THAT SOICHIRO HONDA FOUNDED THE HONDA MOTOR CO. LTD., THE GERM CELL FROM WHICH HIS EMPIRE WOULD GROW, HE LAID THE CORNERSTONE FOR THIS CORPORATION IN THE DIRECT AFTERMATH OF THE WAR BY FOUNDING THE HONDA TECHNICAL RESEARCH INSTITUTE. THIS WAS A SMALL LABORATORY (JUST 172 SQUARE FEET IN SIZE) THAT HONDA WAS ABLE TO AFFORD THANKS TO THE SALE OF HIS PISTON RING FACTORY. HE KNEW WHAT PEOPLE WANTED MOST OF ALL AT THAT TIME: MOBILITY.

In 1950 Honda opened its first sales office in the Chuo-ku district of Tokyo

Establishment of the new company was based on his recently gained knowledge that individual mobility would be one of the key words of the future.

Determined as ever, Honda began work. By November 1946, everything was set to go. The first Honda engine ran – "even if had taken a thousand desperate experiments" – and from 50 cc produced the modest but healthy output of 0.5 horsepower. Although this two-cycle engine (like the modified Army engines that preceded it) created heavy clouds of exhaust – particularly when it was run on gasoline diluted with spruce resin – this did not bother the customers much. The main thing was being able to buy a vehicle that gave them their long-desired mobility.

When production began in March 1947, "they almost beat my doors down. That's how high the demand was." Honda began making 300 two-cycle engines per month, but – in order to increase capacity – had to set up a new factory very rapidly in Nogushi to meet the demand, which had already reached 1,000 engines per month.

As already mentioned, Honda possessed the gift of sensing changes in the market at the right time. He knew that incomes were slowly but surely rising and would lead to higher demand. He therefore drew the necessary conclusions and decided to build a motorcycle. He entrusted its design, logically enough, to a young, unencumbered engineer whom he recruited directly from the Hamamatsu Institute of Technology: Kiyoshi Kawashima.

While Kawashima set about designing the first motorcycle and its engine (to be called the Type A), Honda was already thinking ahead and working hard on a version of the existing engine bored out to 90 cc. This was used for the Type B, with three wheels and a load platform, which in due course became the primary means of transportation for people building up small businesses – and a sensational market success.

It was therefore no surprise that the young company became the market leader within just a few months. After the factory in Nogushi had started up, Honda had a 66 percent share of the domestic market by October 1948. The successful businessman was then able to liquidate his Technical Research Institute and found the Honda Motor Company, Ltd. with an initial capital of one million yen (in current terms, barely 5,000 dollars).

Successful as 1948 certainly was for Honda, it was easily surpassed by the following year. In many respects, 1949 was to be a truly momentous year for the young company. In August, the Honda company was able to present its first Dream motorcycle, which had a 3 hp two-cycle engine of 98 cc displacement. The most interesting detail on this motorcycle was the pressed-steel frame, which Honda had developed after extensive testing, since the frames that had been used up until then regularly broke apart under load (mopeds and motorcycles mainly being used at that time for transporting considerable weights).

Many legends concerning the boss arose over the decades. One of them concerns the name of the "Dream," Honda's first motorcycle of its own design, which was referred to as Type D within the company. After the initial test rides had gone well, the boss and his closest staff members celebrated the success with Doburoku, a strong, sharp rice spirit. Honda remembers: "A somewhat tipsy employee, who had not been following our search for a name attentively at all, suddenly cried out: 'This must be a dream!' The reaction was unanimous: We had found our name. This first motorcycle was called the Dream – the motorcycle of our dreams. The name fitted in perfectly with my childhood fantasies of speed. The embodiment of this first dream was to be followed by an entire series. I was very satisfied with the symbol."

The first job facing Takeo Fujisawa, who was taken on by the company in October 1949, was to bring order into the chaotic sales situation. Honda had not only started to produce two engines and a complete motorcycle, but also sold its engines to other manufacturers who equipped their frames with the Type A and Type D engines. Fujisawa tackled the

problem by forcing his dealers to commit themselves to selling bikes from one manufacturer only.

Fujisawa also had a second problem to solve: "We needed a four-cycle engine. Our two-cycle engines were unpleasant to listen to and also smelled bad." The consequences were clear: despite certain reservations, Honda and his engineers had to develop a four-cycle engine. In November 1949, the capital was increased to two million yen. "Since, by Japanese standards, we were much too young, we had to exert a lot of persuasion to get support from the banks." The following year, the decision was made to move to Tokyo. Fujisawa became Sales Director and opened the office in the Japanese capital in March 1950. In September, the

It took Honda only a few years to become one of Japan's largest motorcycle manufacturers; in July 1953, monthly output had already reached 25,000 units

cornerstone was laid for a new factory in Tokyo, and by November, motorcycle production had begun there as well.

In July 1951, development of the urgently awaited four-cycle engine had progressed far enough for the first test rides to take place. The Type E Dream, created in just six months, had a swept volume of 146 cc and produced 5.5 hp. Test rider Kawashima left Mr. Honda and Mr. Fujisawa, who were following in a car, in his dust. In the mountainous terrain around Hakone – riding up the passes – he reached average speeds of almost 70 km/h (43 mph).

In October 1951 production of the Type E motorcycle began. Despite its relatively high price, it led to a rapid increase in output. The record stood at 130 motorcycles per day. Thousands of salespeople were on the road for the Honda company, propagating the new campaign slogan: "A joy to make, a delight to sell, a pleasure to buy." Honda explained the motto as follows: "Everyone who had a part in our work profited in some way: the engineers who drew up the plans, the mechanics whose good work ensured our success, and finally the consumers, whose daily lives were made just that little bit better by industrial progress."

In 1952, Honda wanted to fulfill another dream: "I was obsessed with the idea of designing a bicycle engine that would be fru-

gal, practical, and popular." After a few months, the initial prototype was finished. The first Model F took to the road in March. It was a simple bicycle with a 50 cc engine attached to the left side of the rear wheel. The engine was painted red, the little fuel tank located above it was in white – a fresh, youthful sight. In June the Cub – as it was officially called – was launched, and by December the production capacity of 7,000 units per month had already been reached. With his two models, Honda had now gained a market share of 70 percent.

The rise to the top could not be stopped. One Honda factory after another came into existence. The newly built "Sumiyoshi" factory in Hamamatsu (July 1953) was soon able to deliver as many as 25,000 engines per month. In parallel to this, Fujisawa wrote to 55,000 bicycle dealers in Japan, of which 30,000 were interested in a cooperative partnership (13,000 of which the sales manager considered substantial enough to sell the Honda company's products).

More and more factory facilities were set up: In March 1954, the Aoi factory in Hamamatsu was dedicated, and soon after, the first proving ground went into operation. This was also the month in which Honda first appeared on the motor sport scene. The first race for which the company entered took place in Brazil. In June 1954, Soichiro Honda watched the legendary Tourist Trophy race on the

Isle of Man, and then toured several European automobile factories. From November 1955 on, an official Honda works team competed in races for the Japanese Motorcycle Championship. This not only satisfied Honda's passion for motorcycle racing,, but also made a tremendous contribution to the popularity of his brand.

In 1956, the capital was increased to 120 million yen; by May 1957 it was already 360 million yen; just one year later it had reached the almost incredible figure for that time of 720 million yen. These are just a few figures that help to give us a picture of the dynamism with which the company grew.

Since the history of Honda motorcycles will be narrated elsewhere, we can limit ourselves here to a brief outline of the years that fol-

In this small building in 1959 the company established the American Honda Motor Co. – now among the largest manufacturers of engines in the world.

Following the European Honda Motor Trading Company, established in Hamburg in 1961, Honda Deutschland became an independent company with headquarters in Offenbach in the Spring of 1968

lowed: In 1959, Honda entered a European race for the first time. Its sixth place in the Tourist Trophy on the Isle of Man in the 125 cc class attracted attention in Europe to the Honda marque for the first time. In June of the same year the Honda Motor Co. was founded in America. This was the sales sub-

sidiary that made the little Honda motorcycles so popular in the USA during the 1960s, when the Beach Boys topped the charts with 'Little Honda'.

In 1961, two other important events occurred (apart from the inevitable increase in capital, which was now 8.64 billion yen): the

THE RISE TO THE TOP BEGINS

first victory in the legendary Tourist Trophy race (which immediately caught the attention of the world's motorcycle enthusiasts) and the first European bridgehead. In June of that year the European Honda Trading Co. Ltd. was founded in Hamburg, Germany. It was later to become Honda Germany, which is today based in the town of Offenbach.

Soichiro Honda, the man who fought against trade barriers right from the very start and loathed protectionist measures, had begun exporting his products early. The first Dream motorcycles were exported to the Philippines in October 1952, and in 1958, the first two motorcycles were sold in the USA. In June 1959, Honda USA was established and was able to sell 96 machines by the end of the year, after which the figure climbed rapidly to 140 motorcycles per month. In 1962, Honda already had a 50-percent share of the motorcycle market in the USA: 65,000 Americans had chosen a Honda motorcycle.

On June 2, 1961 plans matured in Europe and the European Honda Motor Company was added to the trade register in Hamburg. One of Soichiro's closest colleagues was selected to establish the first sales branch in Europe: Noboru Okamura. Just how successful he was as time passed can not only be seen in the European subsidiaries' turnover, but also from the fact that Okamura later (after returning to Japan) rose to be Chairman of the Supervisory Board.

Hamburg's task was to coordinate sales channels and develop a conquest strategy for the individual countries of Europe. For this reason, the Hamburg office was really just a central point from which the individual sales subsidiaries evolved in the years that followed: for instance the N.V. Honda Motor S.A. in September 1962 (out of which Honda Belgium arose). This company built a factory in which mopeds were assembled for the European market; work began in May 1963. Less than a year and a half later, Honda France S.A. was founded in Paris, and in September 1965, Honda U.K. Ltd. began operations in London – other European countries then followed in rapid succession.

In other parts of the world, progress was similarly dynamic: the Asian Honda Motor Co. Ltd. in Bangkok (October 1964), an assembly plant belonging to it (April 1966), cooperation with Mexican and Spanish motorcycle manufacturers (August 1968), and the founding of Honda Australia Pty., Ltd. in Melbourne (February 1969) and Canadian Honda Motor Ltd. in Toronto (March 1969) are evidence of the company's amazing upward trend.

Nevertheless, things did not run perfectly for Honda in Europe at the start. The company had counted on sales of its big motorcycles without realizing that this class required an extra driver's license that many younger

THE RISE TO THE TOP BEGINS

For almost 30 years Civic models have been among the world's most successful compact cars; more than 11,500,000 have already been produced

customers did not yet have. Nor did the bikes' styling appeal to European tastes. Soichiro Honda: "We thought Europe was an old, somewhat antiquated continent and wanted to conquer it with the same model we had used five years before in the New World. We were naïve and did not know today's Europe. Basically, we had learned too much European history and could not imagine that Europe had also embraced progress."

In its first fiscal year (1962/63) the Honda subsidiary in Hamburg had an overall turnover of 6,577,000 German Marks (DM), of

which DM 5,976,000 came from the sale of motorcycles, the rest from the sale of spare parts. The figures increased rapidly: in 1963/64 the turnover was DM 9,747,000, one year later it passed the DM 10 million mark (DM 10,871,000), and by the time motorcycle turnover first dropped (1965/66) the statistics were being supplemented for the first time by a new product area: the automobile.

In the previous chapter we saw how the Japanese government of the day attempted to establish a monopoly against Honda as an up-and-coming company, and how Honda and his business partner Fujisawa cleverly turned public opinion against this decision. The basic idea behind the campaign was their determination to increase the size of the company, with its rapid rate of growth (and magnificent level of earnings). There were critical voices that expressed the opinion that it would be better to diversify by establishing a second leg for the company to stand on outside the engine and technology area – but Honda and Fujisawa energetically opposed such considerations. They wanted to remain loyal to the engines to which they owed their rocket-like rise to the top.

Although Honda's indignation was justified and the Japanese government must surely be thankful today for the stubbornness of the man from Hamamatsu, the fact that one person had dared to oppose the government (and

particularly the Ministry for Commerce and Industry) was held against the company for a long time. Once again, Soichiro Honda had refused to stick to the rigid, immutable rules. He had dared to question a decision made by the government, to get the public on his side, to make a protest. And wasn't this Honda the man who had already earned far too much money while still much too young (and even presumed to display his wealth in public)? Was this not the man who had gone to university at the age of thirty and been asked to leave without taking the exams? The man who had rudely circumvented the government's fuel rationing by producing spruce-tree oil, thus making the authorities look foolish? Was this not the same man who put young men fresh from university into top positions much too rashly? In short: Soichiro Honda had again shown himself to be an individualist, a suspicious act right from the start in a country where team spirit is valued above all else.

That is why in Japan, Honda is still considered to this day an unusual business operation. The share of its budget spent on research and development is disproportionately large, and good engineers rise to positions of auth-

In 1973 Honda surprised the American public and the country's automobile industry with the Civic CVCC, the first car to comply with the strict 1974 exhaust emission laws a year before Honda's competitors succeeded in doing this

THE RISE TO THE TOP BEGINS

With its first portable power generators, Honda opened up another business area. At the same time, one subsidiary after the other was established all over the world: Following Canada and Australia came Honda Motor do Brazil, Ltd. in Sao Paulo – over the years, Honda's network of sales offices and production facilities grew steadily throughout the world.

One decisive date was in June 1972, when Honda launched the Civic, the car that took the company's name around the world millions of times over. The Civic, which is still part of the product program today (in its sixth generation), also wrote technological history with the first transverse power unit and front-wheel drive in this class, since it went into series production before the VW Rabbit (Golf). To date, more than eleven and a half million of these models have been produced, and it has gained the most prestigious prizes and awards around the world.

In October 1953 Honda began to manufacture portable generating sets for agricultural users – this is the Type H

ority much more quickly there than at other manufacturers.

In the 1960s, the Honda company slowly began to crystallize into the form that we know today. With the S 800 Coupe, it established itself as a manufacturer of technically advanced vehicles. At the same time it began to enter for Formula 1 races: Richie Ginther was able to win the Mexican Grand Prix on October 24, 1965, and John Surtees the Italian Grand Prix in Monza on October 10, 1967.

The fact that Honda views itself today as an international company with roots in Japan is clearly the achievement of Soichiro Honda, who began vehemently implementing his "Think global, act local" slogan at an early stage. It is based on the insight that a company with international operations can only be successful if it plans its worldwide strategy centrally, but implements it individually at the local level – in other words, directly in the markets. Logically enough, plans were made early on to set up production facilities around the world. They not only helped to avoid any protective customs duties that might otherwise have had to be paid, but also (as was the case in the USA) to eliminate cultural barriers. In the United States, Honda is considered almost an American company – and the Gold Wing, of which more than a million have been assembled at the factory in Marysville, Ohio, is accepted as an American motorcycle. It therefore comes as no great surprise that today, Honda also exports cars produced in the US (and motorcycles produced in the US and Italy) back to Japan.

This strategy is a key to the decision made in December 1979 to produce a car together with British Leyland Ltd. – developed by Honda and built at Leyland. The first rumors of a contract of this nature spread as early as 1979. On April 4, 1979, the Süddeutsche Zeitung, a major South German newspaper, reported: "British Leyland plans to cooperate with Honda." And continued: "This could give the Japanese industry a decisive breakthrough in the European car market – at a time when the EC Commission is considering restricting Japanese imports. It is only for political reasons that, until now, Japanese carmakers have told the British industry that they are willing hold back and not further expand their 11 percent share of the car market in that country."

Honda liked to be photographed at the wheel of his cars – he knew that such pictures would go round the world and generate good publicity

THE RISE TO THE TOP BEGINS

The joint product began its career in Great Britain on October 7, 1981 as the Acclaim. The Acclaim was a development of the Honda Ballade – based in turn on a variation of the Civic. It was the first model to emerge out of this partnership, which did not end until the spring of 1994, when BMW took over Leyland, or Rover as it had become by then, in a surprise move, and Honda was no longer prepared to work with the new company.

In recent years, the people at Honda have, of course, paid special attention to the strategically interesting (and rapidly growing) markets of Asia. In 1992, for instance, the first contract was signed with a motorcycle production facility in China, and one year later, the Honda Motor (China) Co. Ltd., was set up with headquarters in Hong Kong. In Korea, a cooperative partnership was negotiated with Daewoo.

No mean achievement: After just 50 years, Honda is now the world's largest motorcycle manufacturer (the company's 100-millionth motorcycle rolled off the production line in November 1997) and the seventh largest car manufacturer. It manufactures its products in 95 factories in 34 countries. Each year, more than ten million cars, motorcycles, scooters, and other products such as power generators, lawn mowers, rotary snowplows, and tractors leave the factories – in more precise figures, almost 2.4 million cars, 5.4 million motorcycles and scooters, and 2.9 million "other

products." The figures include articles manufactured in Honda factories under another label. Today, Honda is the world's largest manufacturer of internal combustion engines, and its products find more than ten million buyers each year.

Proud figures, achieved when all is said and done by the imagination and determination of a man who fifty years ago decided to give the people of his country a new chance of personal freedom and mobility.

TELL IT AGAIN, JOHN

I SIMPLY COULDN'T BE
INDIFFERENT TO THAT TIME
AT HONDA. IT WAS MAKE OR BREAK
FOR OUR PROJECT.

TELL IT AGAIN, JOHN

Honda entered Formula 1 racing in 1964 with the RA 271 – but it was at first too heavy and not powerful enough to have any chance of success

An interview with John Surtees, conducted in the summer of 1998.

1966. SURTEES WAS 32 AND WANTED TO BE WORLD CHAMPION.
The fact that he had been world champion eight times before (seven times on a motorcycle, once in Formula One for Ferrari), meant little at that moment. There was no craving on his part for a well-deserved quieter life. John Surtees had the feeling that everything – almost everything – was still ahead of him.

He had put the previous year's accident (Canada, sports-car racing, a very lucky escape), behind him. Observers agreed that from this time on Surtees looked distinctly older than he actually was. (This gave him a chance to turn the clock back in later years: at 64 the sparkle in his eyes outshines most people of 24.)

Something else he had most definitely put behind him was the family link with Ferrari. They had a lot going for each other, Ferrari (the man, the team and the fans) and Surtees. The 1964 World Championship put a noble seal on that relationship. The old man's sympathetic interest in John's convalescence – he had been operated on several times – had established a depth of feeling not previously there.

"When I left the hospital I felt I was one of the family – and that's when I'm at my happiest."

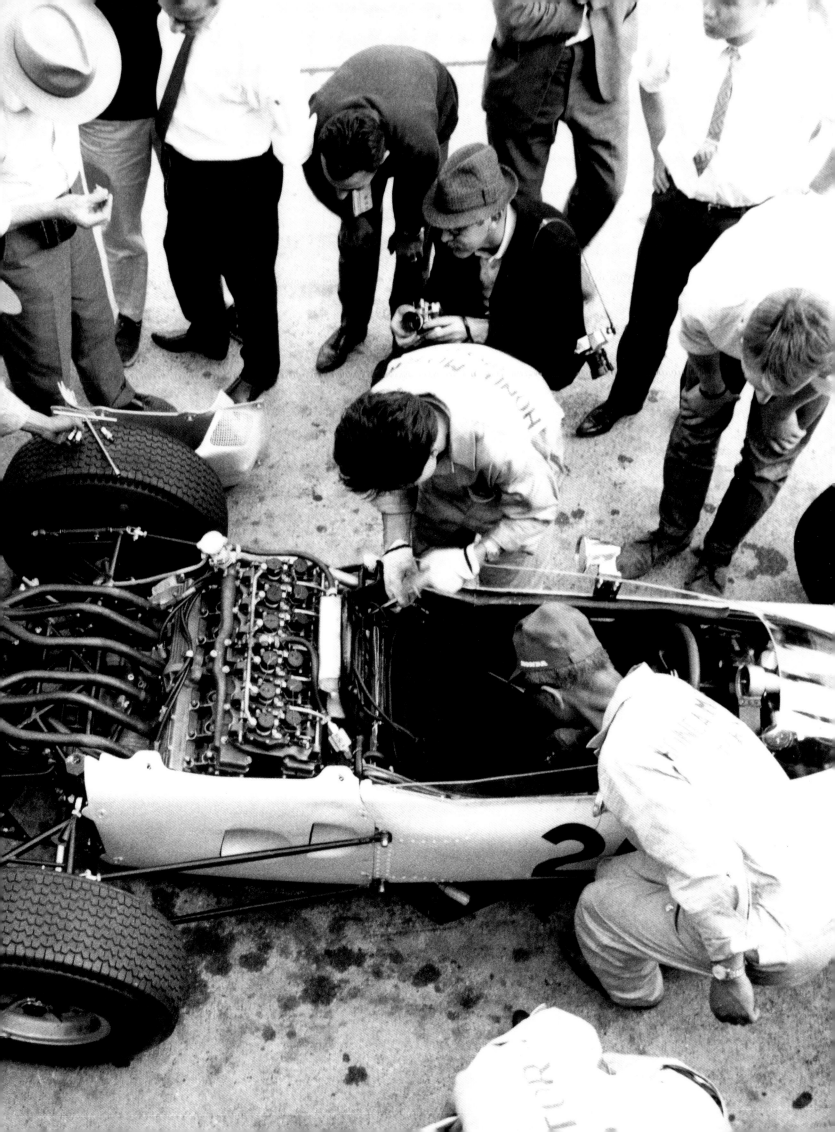

A final check by the mechanics, and the RA 300 is on its way to giving John Surtees and Honda victory in Monza after a dramatic race in 1967

But then, as so often happened at Ferrari, politics reared their ugly head, driving human beings and their mutually defined objectives apart, and of all the well-known altercations between Ferrari and its star drivers, the moment when John Surtees quit Le Mans – before the start of the 1966 race – was the best publicized one of all.

He spent the rest of the season driving for Cooper – and he was upset.

"I was convinced that I would be staying with Ferrari for the rest of my life, but suddenly my world was torn apart."

In Monza, Surtees crossed the line only half a car-length ahead of Jack Brabham

TELL IT AGAIN, JOHN

*Everything was orga-
nized the way Big John
wanted it. Honda gave
John Surtees – here
with team manager
Yoshio Nakamura –
every possible support*

1966. IT WAS HONDA'S THIRD YEAR IN
FORMULA 1, a declaration that the well-
known motorcycle manufacturer was now
venturing onto the automobile scene, even if
this was done at first using cylinder sizes
taken from its motorcycle experience.

The first chapter of Honda's Grand Prix
history was, to put it mildly, slightly un-
orthodox. The team discovered the largely
unknown American Ronnie Bucknum and
hired him as a driver. Ronnie was certainly

okay, but it was the second American in the
team – in this case a top-notch driver – who
chalked up the first victory: Richie Ginther in
Mexico, 1965.

The winning car was immediately condemned
to become a museum relic, because from that
time on the rules were altered, doubling the
maximum engine displacement to 3 liters.
This change brought an entirely new generation of Grand-Prix cars with it, cars clearly beyond anything which Honda had so far
produced.

With the resources of the time, which were
distinctly modest, the 3-liter car only got off
the mark slowly; indeed by the end of the
1966 season it had taken on the appearance
of an endangered species. The project was
underfunded, confidence in Japan was at a
low ebb and the outlook was distinctly bleak.
Enter John Surtees.

"I WAS ON THE LOOKOUT FOR A NEW
FAMILY. I hated moving around from team
to team. For this reason, the most important
factor for me when joining a new team is its
perspective. I'd seen how much Honda had
achieved with its bikes, and I had a lot of faith
in that. If you can make it there, you can
make it anywhere. The intake of Honda
engineers was very similar to that of the Mercedes team when they dominated motor
sport. The company had a strong technical
background. So I thought to myself: this is a
new beginning, something big could develop
from this and I'll be part of it."

Maybe it was destined to be big one day, but it started off in a very, very small way. This at least had the advantage that the emotional ties were very strong. Without Surtees there was a danger that Honda would withdraw from motor sport altogether. He had to take on many different roles: racing driver, technician, organizer, indeed they even asked him to contact potential team sponsors. One thing was clear, this would be a one-car team. Everything was aligned towards Big John.

"Formula One at Honda was the responsibility of Yoshio Nakamura. He was an enthusiast in the truest sense of the word, with the strength to believe in the future. I had a workshop close to London, in Slough, where I maintained my CanAm cars. This is where we set up the Honda racing department, recruited a secretary and two experienced English mechanics, bought a transporter and employed someone to drive it. Three men came over from Japan. These were the spe-

John Surtees and Honda took the RA 301 to the starting line for the Mexican Grand Prix, their last Formula 1 race in the 1960s; not until 1983 was the company to enter this top motor racing category again

51

TELL IT AGAIN, JOHN

cialist mechanics, top people, and "good lads". Nakamura was the link between Japan and Slough."

IT WAS A WONDERFUL ERA FOR FORMULA ONE, with some of the more astute colleagues even calling it "the last days of innocence". There were young men of the caliber of Jim Clark, Bruce McLaren, Jackie Stewart, and Jochen Rindt; there was the elegant Graham Hill and the canny Jack Brabham, and money was a long way from being the number-one topic. The top teams were Lotus, Brabham, Ferrari and Cooper, and the debut of the compact Lotus-Cosworth car heralded the dawn of a new age.

To put it politely, the Honda V12 was an exceptionally powerful design. It was also the heaviest car around, weighing in at 730 kilograms, an amazing 230 kg above the regulatory minimum weight.

Looked at in retrospect, it is quiet unthinkable that a car carrying such a handicap would even consider lining up at the start today. How did they cope with such a situation in those days?

"Naturally, the essential element was the V12 engine. It developed somewhere in the region of 400 horsepower, which was an essentially soothing thought. The situation was obvious. The technology for top performance from Honda at this time could only come from its motorcycle tradition, in other words, from the typical Honda axiom: pro-

duce the power. In the beginning there was power, the rest would be built around it."

John Surtees continues: "I see it this way: at some stage Mr. Honda said: 'Okay, if it has to be a V12, it must have everything we're good at'. Who, in the light of his success story, would have dared contradict him? This not only meant cylinder heads for high engine speeds, but also roller bearings, a central power takeoff, a three-shaft gearbox, and one thing led to another in a logical kind of way. The overall result was a mighty – but a heavy – source of power, and you can't just install that in an ultra-lightweight chassis."

1967's white Honda was, in spite of its robust character, a visually balanced racing car, given a dramatic accent by its raised, centrally located exhaust system. More friendly written descriptions called this a "viper's nest" or an "engine trying to inhale an octopus". The Honda sound was extremely easy to distinguish, to say the least. How can one best describe it?

"Exciting, hoarse, penetrating, harsh, loud, without the generous, soft undertone that I'd been used to at Ferrari. Back then everything at Honda was geared to producing a top-end engine. This resulted in a special sound, which was amplified by all those exhaust pipes with their megaphone ends. It's something I'll never forget. I occasionally have to ask people to speak slightly louder so that I can understand them; I put that down to Honda. They took part of my hearing away."

But surely, they used ear plugs back then? "Well I never had any. I may, at the very most, have used cotton wool. I just loved listening to the engine. Most motorcyclists are like that, they need this close contact with the engine, because that's what they work with. Years later I was given an opportunity to ride Mike Hailwood's famous 500 cc bike, and sure enough it made the same noise as I'd been used to in my Formula One car."

At the start of the 1967 season Nakamura came up with the motto: "Later on we'll get some good parts, and if we are a little bit more successful Japan will support us more." However, sometimes there wasn't even enough money to ship the engine back to Japan for major servicing. This was why

Honda had to miss the French Grand Prix, for instance. But the weight remained the principal problem.

"When the results began to make it clear that something had to change, I made the proposal in the middle of the season to build a new chassis, and to do it right here in England, because of the shorter distances involved and my long-standing contact with Lola, who had always managed to pack large Indy-size engines into comparatively light cars. The Japanese agreed to a joint effort, Mr. Sano visited the Lola factory, hundreds of telexes were sent back and forth, and after six weeks we had a new chassis. It was a close thing, but it was ready for Monza. True, it was still a heavy car, but it wasn't soooo heavy."

"It was a very satisfying race" – John Surtees comments on his sensational victory in the Monza Grand Prix

TELL IT AGAIN, JOHN

John Surtees: "I was convinced that together, Honda and I would be the best team in the world – but then Soichiro Honda decided to use air-cooled Grand Prix engines, and after that the whole thing was abandoned far too quickly"

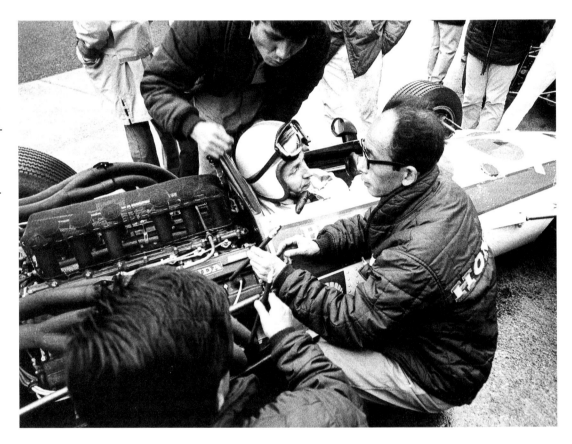

What followed is now racing legend.
On September 10th, 1967 John Surtees won the Italian Grand Prix at the wheel of a Honda with a lead of two-tenths of a second over Jack Brabham. This was one of the most frequently described, heart-stopping finals ever, but we'd like to hear the story again from the Honda cockpit.

TELL IT AGAIN, JOHN.

"We weren't as fast as Lotus, but suddenly there were no more Lotuses left. Graham Hill had left a noticeable oil slick on the inside of the Parabolica braking zone, which the race marshals had covered with cement dust, but we all knew it for what it was: sugared oil!

I was in the lead when we took Lesmo on the last lap. Jack Brabham had sucked himself right up into my slipstream so that I could feel him almost touching the hairs on the nape of my neck, but I knew he would hardly have a chance to overtake me on the fast section leading up to the Parabolica. The Honda's top speed would see to that. After all, we had tuned the car especially for higher engine speeds to suit Monza.

The real problem was a stretch of about 150

meters between the exit from the Parabolica and the finishing line. On this straight section of track, he would be able to out-accelerate me, firstly because he had a more torquey engine and secondly because his was the lighter of the two cars.

I've raced quite a lot of times against Jack, and although he was perhaps the most competitive driver of his day, he certainly was not the type of person to work everything out in advance. People used to say, Jack was the last of the demon brakers, and indeed you quite often saw him approaching a bend with locked-up wheels. As we cut through Vialone and rushed on toward the Parabolica, I decided to give Jack an opening on the inside lane, in other words let him take the ideal line. Jack knew as well as I did that the inside lane had cement dust covering up Graham's oil slick. It wasn't really a trap, but it was an offer on my part. I knew Jack's character really well: if he spotted a space he would go for it.

So I took the center of the track into the Parabolica and concentrated with every nerve-cell in my brain on hitting the very, very, very last possible braking point. In the meantime Jack headed for the inside lane, his wheels were totally locked and he had trouble at first turning in. I braked extremely late, but cleanly, pulled inside and put my foot down to the floor. Jack's wheels finally hit a clean surface, he pulled round and once again he was right there just behind me, but there were only a few meters left, and so instead of shifting up through the gears I decided to leave it in the low fourth gear screaming all the way up to 11,500 revs, and that was enough –half a car length, at the very most!" 31 years later John Surtees put the matter in a nutshell for us:

"It was a very satisfying race."

SATISFYING INDEED, as far as Monza was concerned. Honda and Surtees finished the 1967 World Championship season in fourth place. Not ideal, but none the less equal on points with Ferrari. Now things were expected to really take off. Surtees regarded his long-term perspective as fully confirmed.

Victory at Monza unleashed a wave of enthusiasm throughout the entire Honda clan. Everyone felt that now was the time to move up a gear. The young engineer Kawamoto appeared on the scene and pressed for rapid improvements. Two intermediate stages were agreed on (chassis in England, modified engine from Japan) and two stages for the overall solution: a new, lighter V12, to be installed in a new, smaller car – and this was all planned for the 1968 season.

The intermediate solutions worked, insofar as this was possible with what was still basically a very heavy engine. The re-engineered engine had torsion-bar valve springs and a higher injection pressure; a new exterior feature was that the tortuous exhaust system was now side-mounted.

TELL IT AGAIN, JOHN

Now it definitely was possible to notch up some significant performances, and there were indeed three races which Surtees felt that he could well have won if not for some small idiocy which had occurred when the car was being set up for each race.

"I still looked on this as nothing more than the warm-up phase for the heroic deeds to come. But the music was certainly playing! After many comings and goings of young Japanese we had finally built up an orderly core of experienced people. We grew together and became a genuine team."

Development work on the current car was put on hold, because the racing team was awaiting the new, smaller 12-cylinder engine. Then something strange happened:

"The news from Japan stopped, I couldn't get any information at all. Then suddenly a new car arrived – it was Mr. Honda's car."

Soichiro Honda had personally decided that: "We race what we sell", and that from now on all Honda passenger cars sold should be fitted with air-cooled engines. In October 1968, the Honda 1300 was launched at the Tokyo Show with an air-cooled four-cylinder engine. In the run up to this presentation Mr. Honda had personally halted development of the new 12-cylinder Formula One engine (it was of course water-cooled) and issued orders to build an air-cooled V8.

It was the middle of summer in 1968, and Surtees tested the new car at Silverstone. "It was certainly an interesting exercise.

Interesting in terms of research, but not in terms of a racing car intended to win races soon. The worst thing was the cooling problem. I was told to drive the car at the French Grand Prix in Rouen, but I refused. I considered it unfit for racing conditions, and Nakamura backed me up. Japan replied by ordering the Frenchman Jo Schlesser to drive the car with the air-cooled engine in his local Grand Prix. I returned to my old car."

Rouen in 1968 was to be the bitterest race in Honda's racing history. Schlesser rolled his car and was fatally injured. Surtees: "I don't believe the accident can be blamed on the car. It was a cold twist of fate, the way accidents often are."

Surtees still refused to drive the new car in a race. Did the fault lie in the air-cooling principle or the car's general immaturity?

"In motor sport you have to keep your feet on the ground. The car simply wasn't ready to race. I would have accepted the principle, if it had worked. But I don't believe that an air-cooled V8 without a fan can be raced successfully. Mister Honda certainly believed in the air-cooled principle but as far as I am aware, not a single engineer wholeheartedly agreed with him."

Was there no way that a foreigner, not entangled in the hierarchy, and also of such competent standing and fame as John Surtees, could discuss the matter openly with Soichiro Honda? "No. With the structure the way it was, it simply wasn't possible for anyone to discuss things with him. He was an individual who always kept his distance. Occasionally I had lunch with him, but I was never close to him in the way I was to Enzo Ferrari. And although a critical engineer such as Nakamura believed that he ought to be able to stand up and express his opinion, the contemporary Japanese system prevented him from doing so. One should be seen but not heard, and if you had a different opinion it wasn't your job to air it. This was part of the respect one was expected to have for one's employer. I could understand that, but I was reluctant to do so when it began to prevent us from winning races."

Surtees: "This all happened during the transitory period in which Honda was making the move from being a predominantly motorcycle manufacturer to a car manufacturer in search of a new horizon. One had to appreciate the seriousness of this situation – it was compounded by my immense respect for Mr. Honda as someone who had built up an outstanding company with so much success in the motorcycle area. He was to suffer greatly later on from the mistakes made in racing and in the series production of automobiles based on his own ideas."

THREE SUPERIMPOSED ASPECTS. First: although the accident in Rouen had nothing to do with the car itself, it definitely cast a shadow over the racing program. Second: since everything was concentrated on the air-cooled engine, there were even

more problems in preparing the conventional cars for each race.

The third aspect: air cooling was also causing problems in series-production cars, which resulted in all R+D resources and the capabilities of the Kawamotos and Kumes being devoted to designing a new generation of cars. When these priorities were laid down, the significance of Honda's involvement in motor sport was under threat.

"It was also a tremendously emotional affair", said John Surtees. "My refusal to race the car put Mr. Honda in an extremely difficult situation. There was only one alternative to continuing with the program, and that was stopping it.

After experiencing difficult times with different cultures and the enormous distances involved, I was downcast. This particular time at Honda was something I was simply unable to be indifferent to, it was a make or break situation.

Well-deserved winner's laurels: John Surtees' victory in Monza was one of the greatest surprises in the history of motor sport

*The way a winner
should look: John
Surtees in Monza*

I think a parallel can be drawn between Mr. Honda and Mr. Ferrari. Both had built up their companies and made them into impressive forces by the sixties, but they were also of an age which made it difficult to embark on a search for new designs. Some kind of cross-pollination had to happen. Ferrari wouldn't have been able to go on if Fiat had not stepped in, and Honda would have had to give up if the company hadn't possessed such tremendous resources in its research and development areas."

HAD JOHN SURTEES at any particular moment in that era believed that he could become world champion with Honda?
"That was the whole point. As a racing driver I knew I was as fast as anyone else in the world, and I certainly hadn't moved to Honda simply to try out a new car, but because I believed that together we could be the best in the world. Of course, the bar was raised much higher when Lotus and Cosworth entered the scene. That was another dimension altogether ... but in spite of this I still believe the only thing that Honda lacked was an extra year, and of course the new water-cooled V12 we had been promised. The team's third year would surely have been its championship year.

A major part of my career was centered on dreams. I really did dream of reaching my goal with Honda. Unfortunately, the Honda realignment and the new identity that was intended to make it a force in the automobile world, with specific design features

TELL IT AGAIN, JOHN

which Mr. Honda considered to be right – this just wasn't the most favorable of times for racing. You can be amazingly progressive in technical terms, but if it isn't combined with highly practical considerations you won't be able to put together a package with which races can be won NOW."

What particular satisfaction does he recollect from this time that made it worthwhile for John Surtees?

"All the people that were part of the team back then went on to have terrific careers, Mr. Kume became President, and Mr. Kawamoto later. All our most important mechanics were promoted to very good positions within the company. People who were prepared to sleep on the floor of the workshop in Slough after working all through the night were later able to claim their due honors.

And something else: I believe that the misguided air-cooled Formula One car helped to shorten the period of series-production uncertainty and therefore brought forward the birth of the Civic. Don't forget, this was the launch pad for the fantastic position to which Honda has rocketed on the global automobile market.

So I was a part of something which eventually grew into a very successful story, and this is a tremendously emotional tie which certainly doesn't grow any less significant for me as time moves on."

With twelve cylinders to victory and on to the winner's ceremony in style: John Surtees in Monza

TWO WHEELS CONQUER THE WORLD

THE RAPID GROWTH THAT SOON MADE HONDA THE WORLD'S LARGEST MOTORCYCLE MANUFACTURER STARTED IN A VERY MODEST WAY. AT THE AGE OF 39, SOICHIRO HONDA BEGAN A SECOND CAREER WITH NO MORE THAN A SMALL HUT AND A BATCH OF TWO-CYCLE ENGINES PURCHASED CHEAPLY FROM THE RESIDUAL STOCK OF THE DEFEATED JAPANESE ARMY AS HIS CAPITAL. BUT WITH THESE ENGINES AND TURPENTINE FUEL OBTAINED FROM TREE RESIN, HONDA'S MOTORIZED BICYCLES MEANT MOBILITY AND SUCCESS IN THOSE BARREN POST-WAR YEARS.

TWO WHEELS CONQUER THE WORLD

Two years before the official date, Soichiro Honda set up what was later to become the Honda Motor Company with something of a flourish for those difficult times: the records reveal it to have been a single wooden hut measuring 5 x 3.6 meters on a bombsite in the Japanese town of Hamamatsu. This was in October 1946, and the hut was proudly named the "Honda Technical Research Institute". The small, then still very provincial town, 200 kilometers south-west of Tokyo in the Prefecture of Shizuoka, had been Honda's home for 39 years. This is where he built up his first business as a piston-ring manufacturer, a business which he sold to Toyota after enduring several bombing raids and an earthquake. Hamamatsu would soon be more than just the town from which Honda was aiming to conquer the world motorcycle market. Suzuki and Yamaha were working in the same area east of Lake Hamanako.

In 1946, research effort at the Honda Technical Research was concentrated on Japan's dire lack of transport in general, and of motor vehicles in particular. While engaged in the seemingly impossible task of trying to solve this problem, Honda came across a batch of 500 small stationary two-cycle engines, the last of a military consignment intended for driving generators.

For someone who ten years before had built a racing car with a Curtiss-Wright aircraft engine, combining these two-cycle engines with a bicycle was a task accomplished in no time. This first and probably only design by the master himself was scarcely a milestone of technical elegance, and Honda's early production – now in larger premises – was far from being an example of high efficiency: it sometimes took 12 workers a whole day to put together a working motorized bicycle. Despite this relaxed pace of work, the 500 engines were soon used up.

This news was welcomed by critics of Honda's early efforts to produce motor vehicles, since they thought it wrong to increase the number of motor vehicles on the road when fuel was in such short supply. It was precisely this problem, however, that the Honda Research Institute was tackling successfully by providing postwar Japan with an alternative supply of fuel. Honda extracted turpentine from the trees in a pine wood that he had acquired together with his father, and used it to extend his supplies of gasoline. Although the mixture was not without its problems – the oily additive drastically impaired engine starting and left behind a pungent smell when burned – there was one advantage to this fuel cocktail: the disgusting smell proved to the police that the motorcycle was being run on bio-fuel and not on black-market gasoline.

The 500 army engines were followed by one of Honda's own designs. Like its predecessor, this two-cycle unit with rotary inlet valve had a capacity of 50 cc and a power output

TWO WHEELS CONQUER THE WORLD

of 1 horsepower. Its name, the Chimney Engine, was derived from its weird and wonderful design:, the piston has a tube with transfer ports at the top to control the flow of fresh mixture from the crankcase.

In September 1948, now in possession of its own engine, the company was renamed the Honda Motor Company. The first thing it did was to set about developing a different engine, named the "Model A" rather than the

Honda's first auxiliary bicycle engine design did not reach series production

The Honda Dream E dating from 1951 was the company's first model with a four-cycle engine. Although an immediate bestseller, performance from the 146 cc, 5.5-hp engine was only moderate

"Chimney" to distinguish it from its predecessor, though it still had a rotary inlet valve. The motorcycle fitted with this engine was destined to be Honda's first commercial success. Production continued until 1951 and reached 1,000 bikes a day at its peak.

In 1948, the company began to develop a more powerful two-cycle engine with a capacity of 98 cc, a creditable 3 hp and a two-speed gearbox, bringing it closer to the concept of a genuine motorcycle. In line with this approach, the Model C had a lower-slung, tubular frame and a parallelogram front fork configuration, but retained its pedal cranks and V-belt drive.

The decisive step forward was achieved at the end of the forties with an elegant retro design. The Model D had a pressed-steel frame – similar to the one discarded by BMW ten years earlier for the R 12 – and telescopic forks. The frame again contained the 98 cc engine, but this now had a cone clutch and a kick starter. The bicycle pedals had been replaced by footrests and the V-belt by a chain. Having finally achieved his aim of building a real motorcycle, Soichiro Honda did something that never failed to give him pleasure: he held a party. Even in the early days of the company, this meant a plentiful supply of sake. At the height of the fun, the guests were asked a question: "What should we call it?". When one of the slightly merry guests chipped in with the comment "It's like a dream!" Soichiro Honda reacted spontaneously to this, the first contribution from the company suggestions scheme. "Yes, that's it! We'll call it the Dream".

By the time the Honda Dream D was ready for production at the end of 1949, there was a new man in charge alongside Soichiro Honda, the marketing expert Takeo Fujisawa. With a finely honed sense of customer preferences, he explained to the boss that the metallic sound of the Honda two-cycle engine was unbearable and was holding back sales. It was absolutely essential to produce a refined four-cycle engine as soon as possible. This suggestion found a willing ear and an empty drawing board, at which stood a young graduate of the Hamatsu Institute of Technology, Kiyoshi Kawashima. By the end of May 1951 he had produced the first drawings of a single-cylinder four-cycle engine with a capacity of 146 cc. The first test runs were held around Lake Hakone in the mountains as early as July 15th. The result was not just a more refined sound but more rapid progress, thanks to a power output of 5.5 hp (4 kW).

The production model, the Honda Dream E, had a pressed-steel frame with plunger-type rear suspension; the powerful four-cycle engine initially had to make do with a two-speed gearbox. Three speeds were introduced only in 1953. With this four-cycle engine, the Dream series fulfilled all Soichiro Honda's hopes. Output of the two-cycle bike had been 300 units per month, but this figure had increased almost ten-fold by 1953 at the new Kamijujo factory.

Production figures for the basic models were even better. The Cup F motorcycle with a two-cycle engine, now mounted next to the rear wheel, was rolling off the production line at a rate of 6,500 per month from 1952 on.

The technology of the larger motorcycles was rapidly adapted to match the contemporary European bikes on which they were modeled. The Honda Dream of 1955 had a 250 cc single-cylinder four-cycle engine with overhead camshaft, an output of 10.5 hp (7.7 kW) and a four-speed transmission. The pressed-steel frame had a rear swinging fork with spring struts. However, the real breakthrough came only in 1957, when Honda presented its first two-cylinder model. For the Dream C 70 this four-cycle twin, with its impressive 18 hp (13 kW) power output, was carried in a pressed-steel frame with a sheet-metal leading-link fork at the front and a swinging fork of similar construction with spring struts at the rear. In terms of both style and engineering, the Dream was a continuation of a trend that had made the German

Honda built this Scrambler CL 72, based on its successful CB 72/77 model, as early as 1962 – an early hint of the later fashion for enduro bikes

NSU Max a much sought-after midsize motorcycle in the mid fifties. A year later came the C 72, with electric starter. But the climax was in 1960 with the CB 72 Super Sports. The two cylinder engine now had an output of 24 hp (18 kW) and ran happily up to 9,000 rpm. This extremely willing engine was now mounted neatly in a sporty tubular steel frame open at the front. With this highly successful model, which remained in production for eight years, Honda conquered the world market for sports motorcycles. The CB 72 (247 cc) and the CB 77 (305 cc) had no competitors at this time. There was also their small but equally talented sister, the Honda Benly CB 92 Super Sports, with a 124 cc twin-cylinder four-cycle engine developing 15 hp (11 kW) at 10,500 rpm.

In 1958, Honda came up with a highly capable and, as it was to turn out, extremely far-sighted answer to the problem of mass transport on two wheels. The Super Cup 100, a kick-start moped with leg guards and plenty of space for the feet, became a mega-seller in the years that followed. This unique Honda has been in use ever since, not just in Japan but throughout Asia. And, if the Beach Boys are to be believed, the kids in California were also very keen on it for some time. The 50 cc four-cycle engine with its single horizontal cylinder originally had valves operated by pushrods. Later an overhead camshaft was squeezed into the cylinder head, probably the only significant change in 40 years of production. The Super Cup will no doubt maintain its claim to virtual immortality for many

The opulent curves of Honda's Juno K scooter took the young company into a different business area. The 189 cc, 6.5-hp engine had to propel a weight of 170 kilograms (375 lb)

years to come, since there is no sign of production, now in Vietnam, coming to a halt. In other respects too, this economical engine, which consumes far less than its two-cycle rivals, has proved astonishingly versatile, with versions up to 110 cc driving almost everything on wheels. In addition to conventional motorcycles, this includes the fat-tired three-wheeled ATC bikes.

This small four-cycle engine is also to be found in two timeless "cult vehicles": the Honda Dax, the up-market kick-start moped of the seventies, and the Honda Monkey, the legendary micro-motorcycle used for the last 30 years by world motor racing champions and their entourage to roar around the drivers' compound at the racetrack.

Even in the early days, there were scooters from Honda too. In 1954, when everybody in Europe was riding Vespas, Honda built the Juno K, not exactly a slimmed-down version of the Vespa on which it was modeled. The imposing rear section conceals a potent 189 cc single-cylinder four-cycle engine with an output of 8.5 hp (6.3 kW). The tires are of unique size, namely 5.00-9. Honda's second excursion into the scooter world came in 1962: another Juno, this time with the additional tag M85. The modern elegance of its design is underlined by the use of a 169 cc flat-twin engine developing 12 hp. Interestingly, traces of the Juno K's styling and of the engineering design of the Juno M85 are still to be found on today's Honda scooters for the Japanese market.

After nine successful years, the still-primitive Honda Dream E (left) was followed by the Dream CB 72 Supersports (right). With 24 hp from its 247 cc four-cycle twin engine, it set new performance standards (next double page)

67

Honda conceived the brilliant notion of building a minibike back in 1961. The first Monkey went into production in 1963, and Monkeys are still being built

The Honda CB 750 (right) of 1969 ushered in the superbike era. Its 750 cc four-cylinder engine shocked the world with an output of 67 hp. A more recent equivalent, the CBR 1100 XX Super Blackbird of 1996 (left), with 165 hp from its 1137 cc four-cylinder engine, is a more familiar concept to the present-day rider

Honda's rise to great-power status in the motorcycling world was followed by a brief, rather staid period dominated by the worthy twin cylinders of the CB 250/350/450 series. Then we reach the late sixties, a period when things may have been quiet on the racing front but production was going flat out. In 1968, Honda built and sold 10 million motorcycles.

Before the decade was out, however, the in-dustry was to see yet another engineering tour-de-force from Honda. With the CB 750 F, Honda ushered in the era of super bikes with almost unlimited power. The air-cooled inline four-cylinder engine was to become the symbol of a new performance category. The technical data show that everything that had gone before was just a pale shadow: power surged forth from the 736 cc engine, which was rated at 67 hp (49 kW) at 8,000 rpm. For the first time ever, here was

The Honda Gold
Wing with flat-six
engine as made in
America from 1988
on, is the ultimate
highway cruiser,
with plenty of
power (98 hp/72
kW) from its 1520
cc engine

a road bike capable of approaching the magical figure of 200 km/h (125 mph). And it could brake from high speeds as never before because it had a disc brake at the front.

The 750-cc bike was soon followed by a whole series of four-cylinder machines: the CB 500 F arrived in 1971, the CB 350 in 1972. The designers even flirted with the idea of a four-cylinder 250, but this never got further than initial trials on the test bed, with Soichiro Honda stepping in personally to halt development because of its poor torque curve.

In the late 1960s, when a market opened up in the wild south-west of the United States for enduros of the type ridden in jaw-dropping style by the marijuana smugglers in the film "Easy Rider", Honda ventured into the world of off-road bikes for the second time. The Scrambler CL 72 (based on a slightly modified CB 72) was followed in 1972 by the CL 250 S, a thoroughbred enduro with a single-cylinder four-cycle engine (248 cc and 22 hp (16 kW)) and the moderate weight of 128 kilograms. This was soon followed by the SL 125, a small all-terrain bike developing 12 hp and an affordable toy for grown-up little boys.

Two years later the world was expecting something big and, at the International Bicycle and Motorcycle Show in Cologne, Germany in September, Honda did not disappoint them. With the Gold Wing, Honda offered its customers a full liter of engine capacity. The new superbike, although it was not intended initially as a touring machine, broke new ground technically. It was driven by a four-cylinder horizontally opposed water-cooled engine that ensured ample and sustained power (80 hp (59 kW) at 7,000 rpm) and absolute refinement. Power transmission to the rear wheel by shaft was the logical continuation of this drive concept. The Gold Wing's performance figures were impressive, with a top speed well over 200 km/h and acceleration from 0 to 100 km/h in less than four seconds. But the new Honda broke many a record in other respects too. With a full tank of fuel, it weighed 295 kilograms (650 lb). Although the low center of gravity made this huge weight easier to handle, the Gold Wing was certainly no sports bike. It was only in the course of further development that the bike was able to gain acceptance, acquiring fairings, panniers and a top case to make it a refined touring machine – in the end with six cylinders.

The seventies were an epoch-making decade for Honda, a fact confirmed in 1977 by the appearance of the CBX 1000. Its air-cooled inline engine had six cylinders and established new benchmarks for the superbike: 1074 cc, 105 hp (77 kW) at 9,000 rpm and a maximum speed well beyond 200 km/h (125 mph). The engineering had reached new

levels, similar to those referred to by watchmakers as "la grande complication", with a total of 24 inlet and exhaust valves needing to be correctly adjusted. The engine, which was significantly wider than the handlebars, was immensely powerful but without the silky refinement of the four-cylinder inline engines. Its sound, however, has never been bettered. The power supplied by the six cylinders was not always easy to handle, with the engine constantly trying to prove that it was stronger than the suspension. This conflict negated the new bike's genuine superiority and, for all its power, the CBX 1000 found it hard to compete with bikes powered by slimmer four-cylinder engines. Even a thorough design revision could not rescue the big six-cylinder bike's honor or secure its future.

The specialty in the Honda range in those years was the CX 500, which amazed the world in 1978. For this bike, the design department had once again set itself the task of doing everything differently. Although, very much in line with the times, each cylinder had four valves, they were operated as of yesteryear from a central camshaft by levers, pushrods and rockers. Clutch and gearbox were accommodated underneath the crankshaft in the sump and power was transmitted by shaft as on the Gold Wing. The V engine with an included angle of 80° between the cylinders was refined in operation, despite the non-uniform ignition interval and the extremely short stroke (78 mm bore x 52 mm stroke). It was so flexible that power was available all the way from 1,000 to 10,000 rpm. The 50 hp (37 kW) output was good for a top speed of just under 180 km/h (111 mph). The CX 500 is a very capable

The 82 hp Honda CX 500 Turbo of 1981 failed to appeal to buyers. The turbo-charged engine tended to deliver its power according to an 'all or nothing' principle

machine, though its rather strange appearance hasn't won it many friends. This is indicated by its German nickname: "Liquid Manure Pump". The English are somewhat kinder and refer to it as the "Old Faithful," like some good old reliable friend, which is what the CX was and still is to this day – a reliable touring bike and beast of burden.

In its old age, the CX 500 acquired a new lease of life, with artificial respiration provided by a turbocharger, boosting the power output to 82 hp (60 kW). Unfortunately this was an early turbo design without a waste gate or sophisticated management system. All the power is at the top of the range, with nothing at the bottom. Such racing-bike characteristics force the rider to concentrate extremely hard and give the turbo a bad name, even though modern versions perform much better.

From 1979 on, Honda's top-of-the-range sports bikes began to use four cylinders again. First off the production line – ten years after the original – was the CB 750. An air-cooled inline four, it now had double overhead camshafts and four valves per cylinder. This technical advance did not mean significantly greater power, which went up only slightly to 68 hp (50 kW). The Honda four-cylinder sports bike family grew rapidly. The very powerful 95 hp (70 kW) CB 900 arrived soon after and set the standard for superbikes

in the early eighties, until succeeded in 1981 by the CB 1100 R developing 105 hp (77 kW), the last word as yet in this area.

In addition to the increasingly performance-oriented sports road bikes, the enduro began to gain significantly in importance in these years. Honda's strategy in this area was on the cautious side, concentrating on smaller bikes. Up to 1978, the range consisted of the XL 125 and 250. A fully-fledged 500 cc model arrived only in 1979. The enduros set the trend for suspension design at this time, with the two rear suspension struts being superseded by a single central element. Honda provided a state-of-the-art solution for this in 1980. The competition enduro Honda XR 500R was the first to have the Pro-Link system, which puts the spring strut progressively under pressure by means of a lever mechanism. Despite the many patents the company took out, there were soon a number of imitators in the industry. The technology was initially used on enduros but the road machines were not far behind. The last version of the six-cylinder Honda CBX had this progressive suspension layout as early as 1981.

The early eighties also saw the first crop of easy-riding choppers, or to be more precise, cruisers in the original American sense of the word. After a dozen wild years, this represented a return to a more relaxed form of riding pleasure. Honda had a wide selection of models on sale. On the one hand, there were the traditional four-cylinder bikes such as the CB 650 SC or the CB 750 C, which encouraged calm, relaxed riding with their smooth power delivery. For customers with particularly refined tastes there was the CX 500 C, its unusual V engine a particularly noticeable feature. And finally, there was the VF 750 C, its transversely mounted V4 engine providing an indication of things to come in the form of a new Honda model line.

In the very next year a whole fleet of bikes appeared with their cylinders in a V configuration. Introduction of the sporty VF 750 F with its partial fairing saw the beginning of 15 years of rivalry within Honda between V4s and inline fours in the same power category, a situation that clearly stimulated sales. The VF 1000 C Magna with its powerful V4 pointed the way to the modern-style cruiser. The same configuration was available on smaller machines, for example the VF 400 F sold on the Japanese market. But things were also moving on the V-twin front. The VT 500 E was the first of a line of water-cooled twins with three-valve heads, as used for a whole series of Honda machines until the present day.

One derivative of this series, the XLV 750 R Super-Enduro, provided a particularly impressive demonstration of strength. This 220 kg (485 lb) "ship of the desert" with its 61 hp (45 kW) engine and shaft drive was not one of Honda's most successful models, but

mistakes made at this early stage pointed the company in the right direction. In 1987, the initial design matured into the best-selling Transalp, a touring enduro that weighed a mere 190 kg (418 lb), with a 598 cc engine developing 60 hp (44 kW). It served as the basis for wins in the 1989 Paris–Dakar Rally with the Africa Twin, a 742 cc twin-cylinder bike with a power output of 50 hp (37 kW).

Competition between the inline and V4 cylinder layouts was given new impetus in 1987. The air-cooled inline four-cylinder was pensioned off and replaced by a more modern water-cooled engine. There were no longer any significant differences in performance, especially in Germany, where all machines were limited to 100 hp (74 kW). Honda's marketing department defended the continuation of the two-engine strategy by saying that the inline four had a well-established and loyal clientele.

The mid-eighties saw the appearance of some particularly idiosyncratic V engines derived from racing models. A number of production bikes were derived from the two-cycle engine designs that had dominated the track for more than ten years. Production of the MXV 250F, which began in 1984, was short-lived. Its speedy but correspondingly thirsty two-cycle V3 engine with an included angle of 90° between the cylinders produced 40 hp (29 kW) at 9,000 rpm. Just one year later, Honda simplified the design in imitation of its

In 1979 designer Irimajiri adopted oval pistons and eight valves per cylinder as a means of making the four-cycle racers competitive again. This brave idea was not a success, but at least added a new chapter to the history of engine design

World Championship machine and installed a V2 engine, again with an included angle of 90°, in the NS 250R, resulting in a power output of 45 hp (33 kW) at 9,500 rpm. A three-cylinder V engine was also featured on the NS 400R, which remained in production for three years from 1985 on. The two-cycle engine with two vertical cylinders and a horizontal one corresponded in principle to the power unit of Freddy Spencer's World Championship bike except that the civilian version, at 387 cc, is one-fifth smaller than the 500 cc racing version. The power output of this 192 kg (423 lb) model, at 72 hp (53 kW), was highly respectable, as was its fuel consumption, which was just slightly over 10 liters per 100 kilometers (23.5 US mpg).

History was soon to decide that two-cycle engines would remain the privilege of racers, mopeds and scooters. And Honda's scooter business was well established long before these again became fashionable. The Honda Lead was firmly established in the eighties in three versions: a kick-start scooter, an 80 cc lightweight motorcycle and a brisk 125 cc model. With continuously variable transmission and electric starter, the Lead set the technical standard for the new generation of scooters. The Honda Helix touring scooter of this period pointed the way ahead. With a low, more reclined sitting position, it offered standards of comfort unattained by other two-wheelers over long distances. A single-cylinder four-cycle engine developing 19 hp

(14 kW) ensured reasonably rapid progress. The Helix scooter also strengthened the trend towards greater model continuity. Like many other Honda models introduced at this time, it is still around in a more highly developed form.

A change was under way, bringing greater maturity and stability to the Honda model program from the late eighties on. In these times of globalization, it was necessary to strive for greater technical discipline. Honda motorcycles were now being built in various countries, often at significantly lower cost than in Japan. And they were not all designed in Japan either. A development center in the USA took charge of the Gold Wing, which had long since been perceived as an American bike, and transformed it into the perfect roadgoing "pleasure steamer". Similar activities in Europe were the responsibility of Honda Engineering in Offenbach, Germany, which, in line with Old World tastes, developed Honda's best-ever touring machine concept and even found a suitable name for it: Honda ST 1100 Pan-European.

There was room for two rare birds of paradise in this new world order: the NR 400 and the NR 750. These, the most expensive production motorcycles of all time, incorporated a real spark of genius on the part of designer Shoichiro Irimajiri. It was a good ten years ago that Irimajiri came up with the idea of building a V4 engine with oval pistons and

cylinders as a way of coping with the four-cylinder limit in the 500 cc World Motorcycle Racing Championship category. This and the use of eight valves per combustion chamber make the charge cycle more efficient. The result was a technically superior four-cylinder engine, although ultimately one that was still unable to beat the two-cycle designs convincingly on the race track. This oval-piston machine remains a technical cult object. Anyone who wants an NR 750 with its claimed power output of 125 hp may well have to pay more than 50,000 dollars - though this could prove to be a good investment for such a sought-after collectors' item.

Since then, superbikes with conventional pistons have easily overtaken the NR 750's performance figures. An RVF 750 RC 45 in racing trim develops 180 hp (132 kW) at 14,500 rpm with no trouble at all and even among the production models there are now plenty of bikes offering power well beyond the 98 hp "sound barrier" decided upon by German insurance companies. A Honda CBR 1100 XX without an engine governor develops 165 hp (121 kW), accelerates to 100 km/h (62 mph) in 3.1 seconds and reaches a top speed of 265 km/h (165 mph). But genuinely fast riding is no longer the privilege of the powerful, as is clearly demonstrated by a lightweight such as the Honda CBR 900 RR, weighing 187 kg and developing 128 hp (94 kW). Not only does it win the 100 km/h (62 mph) sprint in 3 seconds; motorcycles that are as light as this show no mercy to their competitors on the race track: they stay in front.

The oval-piston Honda NR 750 was actually produced as a limited special edition, though its power output of 130 hp from 747 cc was soon to be surpassed by later superbikes

Honda began to conquer the enduro market in 1972 with the Dream SL 250 S. The company's most spectacular sport successes were in the Paris–Dakar desert rally, with four successive wins between 1986 and 1989

Most customers are inspired by other ideals, however, and these are being met. In the late nineties there was a clear wish for minimization that is no respecter even of superbikes. Four cylinders are no longer the standard by which all things are measured. The Honda VTR 1000 F Firestorm represents this new, more restrained approach, with a 1000 cc V2 engine, an elegant but nevertheless highly dynamic solution providing a power output of up to 110 hp (81 kW).

For those who value comfortable, well-protected riding rather than maximum performance, Honda provides an even wider range of options in terms of the number of cylinders. The new NT 650 Deauville tourer has a 657 cc V2 engine with a power output of 54 hp (40 kW). The long-range Pan European rockets along with its 1084 cubic centimeters and 98 hp (72 kW) from a V2 engine, and the Gold Wing – now well over 20 years old – has for some time had a six-cylinder, 1,520 cc horizontally opposed engine which delivers 98 hp without overdoing the revs.

TWO WHEELS CONQUER THE WORLD

The current "less is more" fashion is having an obvious effect on the aerodynamic clothing of the sports bikes. Riders want to feel the wind again and are perfectly willing to sacrifice a certain amount of speed for it. This has resulted in a new generation of "naked bikes". Some prefer classic shapes such as the Honda CB 1300 Big One, others the brash modern look of the CBR 600 Hornet; others again limit themselves to a single cylinder, as on the Honda SLS 650.

A good third of all motorcycle riders show a determined desire to abandon ultimate speed by choosing choppers or cruisers. They offer the relaxing experience of gliding along on a low-slung machine with the obligatory authentic sound of a large V engine. Honda plays a true classical arrangement on this theme with the twin cylinders of the Shadow (VT 600 C, VT 750 C2 and VT 1100 C2) and develops it – just as it did 15 years ago – on its four-cylinder instrument, the Magna (VF 750 C). Here cruising power is restrained to a modest 52 hp (38 kW), the maximum that the two cylinders of this 1100 cc bike are invited to supply. Those who want to cruise more rapidly have to choose the Honda F6C, known elsewhere as the Valkyrie, which has the Gold Wing's six-cylinder engine installed in its bare tubular frame and develops 98 hp (72 kW) from a generous displacement of one and a half liters.

However, the company has not lost its sense of appreciation for smaller units. At the 1997

World Sales Champion

Honda is by far the most successful make of motorcycle in the world. In the last fifty years, it has built and sold more than 100 million motorized two-wheelers. 58 million of these were manufactured in Japan and a further 42 million by factories in 27 other countries throughout the world. So far 3 million Honda motorcycles have been built in Europe.

Tokyo Motor Show, Honda presented the prototype of a small motorcycle for children. Its tiny engine has a cubic capacity of 31 cc but uses the refined four-cycle principle, just as Takeo Fujisawa would have wished fifty years ago.

Although Honda is not yet at the stage of building only four-cycle engines, a date has already been fixed. From 2002 on, there will be no more two-cycle production machines from Honda. And now it seems that the outdated but powerful two-cycle dinosaurs will not even be preserved on the race tracks of Jurassic Park. In 1998 there was the first hint that the Formula 1 for motorcycles in the next millennium might be for four-cylinder, four-cycle bikes with a displacement of one liter.

FOUR DECADES OF SUCCESS

HONDA'S RACING MOTORCYCLES

I F WE CONSIDER THE EXCITING AND EVENTFUL EARLY PERIOD IN THE LIFE OF SOICHIRO HONDA, IN WHICH FOR MANY YEARS UP UNTIL 1936, THE YEAR OF HIS SEVERE ACCIDENT, THE ENTREPRENEUR AND RACING DRIVER ROARED AROUND JAPAN'S SHORT OVAL RACING CIRCUITS IN A CAR THAT HE HAD BUILT HIMSELF, POWERED BY A SUPERCHARGED CURTISS AERO ENGINE, WE CANNOT HELP WONDERING WHETHER HIS DESIRE TO BUILD MOTORCYCLES AND PROVIDE HIS FELLOW-COUNTRYMEN WITH THE BENEFITS OF MOBILITY WAS NOT MOTIVATED TO SOME EXTENT BY THE DESIRE SOME DAY, IN SOME WAY, TO RETURN TO THE RACING TRACK.

Soichiro Honda had been planning this "comeback" for a long time and with characteristic thoroughness – though on an extremely tight budget, given the fact that the recently established company was not doing particularly well in the early nineteen-fifties. In Japan there was a bitter struggle between many small motorcycle brands that had sprung into existence in the golden age that followed the Second World War and were now going through a recession.

Honda was therefore fairly short of funds in 1954, when he started out on his expedition to the Isle of Man to take part in the Tourist Trophy motorcycle race. Nevertheless, he threw himself into the task, determined to take the World Championship title and dominate the world market one day despite his lack of finances. This undertaking seems amazingly ambitious when we consider the company's engineering resources. His most powerful production machine, the rather elderly Honda Dream 4E with a power out-

put of 8.5 hp (6.3 kW) from 220 cc was just half as powerful as a 250 cc NSU Max, which delivered 17 hp (12.5 kW). Honda was only marginally interested in the large big-name bikes. He noted Ray Amm's victory in the 500 cc category, the Senior TT, won in the rain on the single-cylinder Manx Norton against Geoff Duke on the four-cylinder Gilera, but he was much more interested in the victorious NSU works machines: the 124 cc Rennfox ridden by Ruppert Hollhaus and the 248 cc Rennmax of Werner Haas, winners of their respective categories in the Lightweight TT.

The performance data of the NSU machines reflected the current technical standard clearly and only too alarmingly for Honda. The single-cylinder engine that powered the 125 bike developed 18.5 hp (13.6 kW) at 11,500 rpm, the twin-cylinder for the 250s reached 39 hp (29 kW) at the same engine speed. This was the technology that fascinated Honda – the kind of machines he wanted to carry the Honda name.

The conclusion of Honda's trip to Europe, as described by ex-motorcycle racer Mike Woollett in his book "Honda", clearly illustrates the financial constraints that affected the Tourist Trophy project.

In the 1960s Honda did not take long to reach the top in World Motorcycle Championship events. The team won this title in each of the solo categories except the mighty 500 cc class, where success was only achieved after a second attempt some years later

Tom Phillis, Luigi Taveri and Mike Hailwood were the elite riders who completed the task begun by team manager Kiyoshi Kawashima in 1959 on the Isle of Man

Impressed by the quality and availability of European racing components, Honda had gone on something of a spending spree, buying mainly chains, tires and carburetors. When he tried to check them in at Rome Airport, the counter staff promptly complained about the extreme excess weight of his baggage and demanded appropriate payment. Unfortunately, Soichiro Honda had long since spent the last of his travel allowance. The small wiry figure argued stubbornly that there were heavier people than him and they didn't have to pay for excess weight. According to legend, Honda arrived at a cashless solution to the problem: he took various items of clothing out of his suitcase and wore them one on top of the other to lighten the load.

The close look that Soichiro Honda had taken at the NSU machines proved its worth five years later. In 1959, under the leadership of the engineer and pioneer of the four-cycle engine at Honda, a Honda team with Japanese riders entered the Tourist Trophy for the first time.

The first Honda works bike was a 125. The only essential difference from the NSU Rennfox was that it had two cylinders. Otherwise, the engine was remarkably similar in design. The two overhead camshafts were driven by a vertical shaft and spur gears. The power output of the small twin, at 18 hp (13 kW), was just below that of its engine that had served as its model. Its strength is evident from the rated engine speed of 13,000 rpm. Other details are also reminiscent of the German model, but in 1959 the leading-link forks of the Honda were already well out of date.

In the race for the Tourist Trophy, the Hondas were up against three established makes: MV Agusta, Ducati and MZ. Although Tarquino Provini on a single-cylinder MV won

HONDA'S RACING MOTORCYCLES

the race with a big lead over the Hondas, the three Japanese riders captured the team prize – somewhat to their own surprise – with Naomi Taniguchi finishing seven minutes after Provini to take sixth place and the other two works riders coming in seventh and eighth.

August, two months after the TT, saw the appearance of the Honda RC 160 at the Mount Asame race in Japan. This was a 250 cc racing bike with a four-cylinder engine and suspension that had not been significantly modified. In its basic layout, the power plant was similar to that of the 125 but with the vertical shaft on the right-hand side. It was on this bike that Sadeo Shimazaki won the All Japan Endurance Race.

Starting with the TT in 1960, Honda began to enter other European races with its 125s and 250s. In addition to Taniguchi and Tanaka from Japan, Honda employed a number of riders from the international racing fraternity: the Australians Bob Brown and Tom Phillis, the Rhodesian Jim Redman and the Scot Bob McIntyre. The bikes had been thoroughly updated. Extending forwards from the "dolphin"-type fairing there was now a modern telescopic fork. The aluminum panels concealed a new engine with the cylinders inclined forward, a configuration which improved the flow of cooling air to the cylinder head and lowered the center of gravity. The camshafts were no longer driven by the somewhat outdated vertical shaft but by spur

gears located in the center of the engine, between cylinders two and three. Lubrication was now by dry sump, with a separate oil tank. Honda had also made significant progress in performance. The power of the 125s was claimed to be 21 hp (15.2 kW) and that of the 250s 40 hp (29 kW) and engine speeds had gone up to somewhere beyond 14,000 rpm Honda had decided on four valves per cylinder because of the reduction in moving masses and of course because of the more efficient cylinder filling that could be achieved by that means. Metallurgical research also played its part: each tiny valve weighed just 12 grams or under 20 grams with its bucket tappet.

The Honda racing team in the 1960s was a model of perfect organization. The bikes were superbly prepared, and the best riders in the profession were engaged. It was during this period that Mike Hailwood rose to superstar status

In 1963 Honda built the RC 113 with twin-cylinder engine for the 50 cc class; there were four valves per cylinder and the engine developed 13 hp at 19,000 rpm. The rim-type front brake was rediscovered 30 years later by mountain-bike designers

Despite this technical progress, 1960 was a learning curve for Honda on European racing circuits. Jim Redman and Tom Phillis achieved second places in the 250 cc class and the results in the TT showed improvements in the teamwork area: sixth, seventh, eighth, ninth and tenth places in the 125 cc class and fourth, fifth and sixth places in the 250 cc class.

A year later, all the effort that had gone into research finally brought results: Mike Hailwood entered the record book as the first rider to win a World Championship on a Honda. Mike the Bike, then 21, fulfilled Soichiro Honda's dream of winning the Tourist Trophy with victories in both the 125 and the 250 classes. He didn't even have a contract:

the bikes were on loan. Tom Phillis won the riders' World Championship in the 125 cc class ahead of Ernst Degner (MZ).

1961 was the beginning of a long series of victories for the Honda marque, with 16 World Championship titles for the riders and 18 for the marque by 1967. In 1966, Honda won the manufacturers' title in all five solo classes. In the 50 cc category, however, the rider's title went to Hans Georg Anscheidt on Suzuki and, in the 500 cc category, to Giacomo Agostini on MV Agusta.

These results were the fruit of an uncompromising technical development program which, in the next few years, was to produce power units for all five classes (50 cc, 125 cc, 250 cc, 350 cc and 500 cc). The engine block

was initially the most fertile area. Reducing the cylinder dimensions (bore 44 mm; stroke 41 mm) enabled the engineers to lower cylinder displacement from 62.3 cc to 49.9 cc (bore 40.4 mm; stroke 39 mm) for the smallest class or to increase it to 339 cc (bore 49 mm; stroke 45 mm) for the 350 cc class, according to requirements.

In 1966, faced with increasing competition from two-cycle designs, Honda introduced a whole new generation of racing engines with significantly smaller cylinder volumes, falling into three classes. The smallest were the 24.8 cc cylinder units. Two of these could be combined for the 50 cc class and five for the 125 cc class. With the "mini-pots", specific output climbed to 272 hp (200 kW) per liter.

This meant 34 hp (25 kW) for the 125 cc and 13.5 hp (10 kW) for the 50 cc engines, achieved at crankshaft speeds of up to 20,000 rpm, a figure which strikes fear into the hearts of engineers even today.

In the case of the 50s, which were up against particularly stiff competition from the two-cycles (Kreidler and Suzuki), the engineers sought a solution to their problems in extreme lightweight construction, resulting ultimately in a dry weight of 50 kg (110 lb). This engineering imperative to slim things down led to tire widths of the kind more familiar now on mountain bikes (2.00-18, 2.25-18). Another feature that anticipated such bikes was a front rim brake of a type which 30 years later is all the rage (Shimano V-Brake).

Mike Hailwood won the 1967 riders' world championship on the RC 174, and Honda thus took the constructors' title in the 350 cc class. Although the transverse six-cylinder engine was only a bored-out 250 cc unit with a displacement of 297 cc, its 65 horsepower were sufficient for the title

Development of the 125 cc racing bikes progressed from the twin-cylinder RC 145 of 1962 (left) through the four-cylinder 2RC 146 of 1964 to the RC 149, a 1966 design with five cylinders. Power went up from 24 to 34 hp. From 1962 on, Honda sold the CR 110 as a 50 cc, 8.5 hp club racer

In the middle of the range there were now two wide inline six cylinder racing engines with 24 valves, an awesome figure at that time. For the 250s, the six tiny cylinders (bore 39 mm, stroke 34.8 mm) each had a swept volume of 43.2 cc, for a power output of something over 60 hp (44 kW) at 18,000 rpm. The 350s had a volume of only 297 cc with somewhat larger cylinders (bore 41 mm, stroke 37.5 mm) and rated power was a hefty 65 hp (48 kW) at 17,000 rpm. Another notable feature was the engine's weight: 118 kilograms. The dry sump lubrication system with separate oil tank was sacrificed for the sake of lightness, the oil reservoir being located in the engine block again.

At the top of the range were the 500 cc engines. Because there was more power available from the half-liter swept volume than suspensions and brakes could cope with at the time, the tendency was to use fewer cylinders. MV Agusta had reduced the number to three on its racing engine. Honda decided to use four, each with a generous 124.9 cc and a stroke that was not too short (bore 57.6 mm, stroke 48 mm). An ample 90 hp (66 kW) was claimed for this engine, just half as much as the rider and the rear tire of one the latest 500 cc two-cycle racing machines or four-cycle 750 cc endurance racers are expected to cope with. And although today's riders are happy with the power they have to play with,

Mike Hailwood and Brian Redman always spoke with a certain awe of the 500 cc monster, even though it didn't bring them the world championship.

In the late sixties it was the small categories that posed the technical problem for Honda. The use of two cylinders for the 50 cc bikes and four cylinders for the 125s was no longer enough to hold the powerful two-cycle bikes of Yamaha and Suzuki in check. These rival machines were less complicated technically and more powerful on the track. It was impossible to overlook the fact that the four-cycle engine had reached its feasible development limits. Increasing performance by the use of ever-smaller components and higher engine speeds had inevitably added to the negative characteristics. More moving parts and their speeds meant a sharp rise in frictional losses, while the volumetric efficiency of the cylinders was significantly reduced by the short time available for exhaust and mixture induction. Overall, the engines were less efficient. Engineers demonstrate this objectively by calculating the mean effective pressure, a theoretical value used as a standard for the efficiency of a reciprocating engine. With the trend towards high-speed multicylinder four-cycle engines, mean effective pressures had steadily fallen and any further move in this direction would merely make the situation worse.

Examples show this clearly: the 500 cc four-cylinder, with its 90 hp (66 kW) at 12,000 rpm, has a mean effective pressure of 13.5 bar. A 125 cc five-cylinder engine with a power output of 34 hp (25 kW) at 20,500 rpm manages just 11.9 bar. With twice the number of power strokes, two-cycle engines were developing something just short of this value even then. This led Honda not only to abandon a project for a three-cylinder 50 cc engine but in 1967 to withdraw completely from the two smallest World Championship categories.

History shows that this was the beginning of a complete withdrawal, as the superiority of the two-cycle engines, which produce power from every revolution of the crankshaft, made itself felt in the larger engine categories too. At the end of the 1967 season, the company decided to withdraw from official participation in the motorcycle world championship. In any case, Honda's plans were by then different and more ambitious, with greater concentration on Formula 1 motor racing.

That did not mean Honda had given up motorcycle racing entirely. Moto-cross was very much on the way up, especially in the USA, where Honda's Japanese competitors were already successful. Honda management therefore decided to show the flag in moto-cross in the important American market.

War between the two-cycle and four-cycle principles had already broken out on the rough moto-cross circuits. Although four-cycle bikes were still competitive in the late sixties, the upsurge of the two-cycle principle was obvious and clever engineers such as project leader Soichiro Miyakochi knew that the advance of the lighter two-cycle bikes would be unstoppable. But this insight conflicted with the prevailing doctrine at Honda, which since its introduction by Takeo Fujisawa – by then a director of the company – had made the four-cycle engine something of a sacred cow – the only valid solution. In 1971, despite opposition from the traditionalists, Miyakoshi was able to push through the two-cycle engine principle, this perhaps being made easier because at about that time Soichiro Honda gave up his position as Head of Research and Development.

The result was – by today's standards – a rather filigree 250 cc moto-cross bike with the very compact CR 250 engine. This power unit heralded the renaissance of the two-cycle engine at Honda and was successful right from the start. The very first production moto-cross machine, the CR 250 M, sold as the Elsinore, was a hit in the USA. Honda's route to success off-road was obviously a lot longer than that on the track, but in 1981, after ten years and many small victories, the company finally made it: the Belgian rider

It's getting started that's difficult. The first Honda racing bike, the RC 160 dating from 1959, weighed 134 kg (295 lb), too much for a 250 with a 35 hp four-cylinder engine. The RS 750D with 100 hp V2 engine (right) was built in 1984 for American sand racing, and defeated Harley Davidson to win the championship

The RC 149 is the ultimate piece of machinery from this period. Its displacement of 124.41 cc is distributed among five cylinders, each of them with four valves.
The resulting 34 hp are developed at 20,500 rpm, with 12 Newton-meters of torque at 19,300 rpm. Luigi Taveri took the world championship in 1966 on this bike, and Honda the constructor's title

André Malherbe became World Champion and was able to take the same the title in the following year as well.

The long road to championship honors reflected the successful implementation of a particular power principle. The Elsinore CR 250M began its moto-cross career in 1972 with an air-cooled two-cycle engine developing 33 hp (24 kW) at 7,500 rpm. Nine years later, the Honda CR 250R production racer had a water-cooled engine. Output had now risen to 41 hp (30 kW) with the rated engine speed unchanged at 7,500 rpm. It is worth noting that twelve years later, in 1984, the RC 125M produced the same amount of power as the 250 cc Elsinore, 33 hp (24 kW), from half the cubic capacity.

Honda was now back on the racing track. The return to road racing had essentially already begun way back in 1969 when the French team of Michel Rougerie and Jean Urdich won the Bol d'Or. In 1970, a CB 750 built with factory components was entered for the classic 200-mile race for production bikes in Daytona; Dick Mann took it to a clear overall victory.

It was only five years later that a more consistent pattern of development for such endurance races emerged in Europe. In 1975, the long-distance classic, the Bol d'Or, held over 24 hours in Le Mans, saw the emergence of a CB 500R with a four-cylinder engine

bored out at the factory to give 749 cc, a four-valve head and a camshaft driven by spur gears. The machine's very first appearance ended in tragedy when Morio Sumiera was killed in a crash during practice. The project was abandoned. In any case, the engine's output of 87 hp (64 kW) at 11,000 rpm was not regarded as competitive even in 1975.

For the next season the company produced a much more radical endurance-racing engine, its four cylinders anticipating the design of the cylinder head with twin overhead camshafts and multi-valve technology that entered production almost three years later. The RCB 1000 of 1976 had a full liter of engine displacement and an ample 120 hp (88 kW) at 9,000 rpm. By 1981, its power output had risen to 130 hp (96 kW). From that point on, Honda racing engines based on this design were to play a significant role in the European Endurance Championship. Successes in the most famous race in the series led the company to name the production version the Bol d'Or.

At the same time strong competition was brewing from within the company. The new generation of water-cooled V4 engines was chasing success not only in the market place but also on the race track. Development, which began in 1982 with the RS 100RW — a 1,000 cc bike developing 150 hp (110 kW) designed for racing in America — soon took on a European dimension. In 1984, the

HONDA'S RACING MOTORCYCLES

Honda RS 750R with a V4 engine and highly impressive 120 hp (88 kW) appeared. Honda's return to Grand Prix racing began in 1979 with a technical miracle. Despite the experience gained with two-cycle engines in moto-cross, the potential world championship machine was to have a four-cycle engine. But all calculations showed that since the late seventies a 500 cc four-cycle would have to have 8 cylinders if it was to have enough power to beat the two-cycle engine with three or four cylinders, and the Féderation Internationale de Motocyclisme (F.I.M.) had already ruled out such a battle of the cylinders by limiting the number that could be used: a single cylinder up to 125 cc, two up to 250 cc and four up to 500 cc.

This led engineer Irimajiri to consider an engine that would have the short stroke of the eight-cylinder engine – advantageous for high engine speeds – and its large valve cross-sections for optimum cylinder filling. The result was the Honda NR 500 with a V4 engine that duplicated the geometric conditions of a V8 engine with large oval cylinders. The cylinder liners and pistons had the unconventional bore dimensions of 93.4 mm x 41.1 mm which, combined with a stroke of 36 mm, yielded a displacement of 499.5 cc. Performance data were not particularly promising: the official figure was over 115 hp (85 kW) at 19,000 rpm. Torque was not dramatically high either: 45 newton-meters at 16,000 rpm. However, the useful engine-speed range

was quite respectable for a racing engine. On the other hand, the NR 500 had another problem compared with its rivals: at 130 kilograms it was relatively heavy. The well intentioned bid to restore the honor of the four-cycle engine in the 1980 season was a failure. The two-cycle engines of the competition were faster and more reliable. And even the brief appearance of a higher-capacity oval-piston engine, the Honda NR 750 with a power output of 155 hp (114 kW) at 15,250 rpm, in the Endurance World Championship did nothing to justify this revolutionary principle. The machine got no further than the 24-hour race for motorcycles in Le Mans, where it broke down and disappeared for ever from the annals of history.

Having learned from this experience, the racing department at Honda now focussed its attention firmly on the two-cycle principle. This provides a power stroke for every revolution of the crankshaft and can produce high power at far lower engine speeds. For racing two-cycle engines, extreme stroke and bore dimensions are neither necessary nor desirable. Cylinders with a displacement of 124.8 cc, which would soon be the standard on Honda grand prix machines in all three categories, could be produced using a 54 mm bore and a 54.5 mm stroke, as on the production model.

Initially, the NS 500 of 1982 had a V3 engine with somewhat larger cylinders, giving

The Honda RCB 1000 Endurance racer dating from 1976 still has a slightly improvized look. In contrast, the NSR 500, with which Michael Doohan and Honda have collected 500-cc their world championship titles almost as a matter of routine in recent years, is a highly professional piece of work (next double page)

HONDA'S RACING MOTORCYCLES

120 hp (88 kW) at 11,000 rpm and 79 Nm of torque at 10,500 rpm. It also weighed significantly less than 120 kilograms.

By 1982 Honda was back on the winning track with the NS 500. After an intermission lasting 15 years, the American Freddy Spencer won the World Championship. From then on it was just like the old days, with Honda competing in all three solo categories of a slimmed-down World Championship. True to tradition, Honda began to win trophies once again. Since 1983, Honda has won another 16 World Championship titles: three for the 125s, five for the 250s and eight in the premier 500 class. The most successful rider and three-times champion was Freddy Spencer, ahead of Mike Doohan, although the latter has won the title four times in the last few years.

At first glance, the technology of the two-cycle engines did not change dramatically over fifteen successful years of racing. The change from the three cylinders of the NS 500 to the four of the NSR 500 in 1985 was the first small but fundamental modification. The four cylinders in V formation, each with a standard capacity of 124.8 cc, provide greater power and performance: 140 hp (103 kW) at 11,500 rpm with torque in the region of 90 newton-meters. The increase in the number of cylinders called for a revision of the design. The three-cylinder bikes had had one crankshaft and therefore one crank-

case, while right from the start the four-cylinders were a combination of two twin cylinders with two crankshafts in two separate crankcases. This allowed the engineers a large degree of freedom in adapting the included angle between the cylinders to the installed conditions. Instead of the 90 degrees that were theoretically advantageous, angles of around 110 degrees were adopted. Although this does not permit correct balancing of masses and a uniform ignition sequence in all cases, these are not essential on racing machines.

On the contrary, the first half of the nineties showed that uniform power flow is not necessarily the ideal in racing. In 1994 two four-cylinder designs went head to head at Honda: the Screamer, with a uniform ignition sequence at intervals of 90 degrees, and the Big Bang, where two power strokes occur with just 80° between them and are then followed by a longer interval. The advantage of this unconventional design is that it produces power at defined intervals, thereby reducing wear on the rear tire, which is severely loaded in any case. Even so, the tread has to put down 200 hp (147 kW) onto the road.

In the 1996 season, the Honda four-cylinder 500cc bikes faced competition from a not entirely unexpected quarter, a machine with just two cylinders developed in-house. This trend towards greater economy of means

HONDA'S RACING MOTORCYCLES

arose from the realization that the times achieved by the less powerful but more maneuverable 250s were getting closer and closer to those of their larger cousins. The 499 cc capacity of the twin was obtained by generous dimensioning (bore 68 mm, stroke 68.8 mm), giving a maximum power of 135 hp (99 kW) at 10,250 rpm. Although the four-cylinder was considerably more powerful, with a power output of 200 hp (147 kW) at 12,500 rpm, it was questionable how much of this power could actually be used under real conditions. And when it came to handling, there was a significant difference due to the weight: the two-cylinder weighed 103 kg, the four-cylinder 130 kg. As yet, however, the four-cylinder machines have been able to make good use of their superior power: Mick Doohan has won every World Championship in his class since 1994 on a four-cylinder machine.

Since 1988, the large four-cycle engines have also been entered for the Superbike World Championship. Two engine sizes are allowed in this class: the four-cylinder machines are restricted to 750 cc, the twins are allowed up to 1000 cc. Honda's racing bikes with a 750 cc V4 engine got off to a great start: Fred Merkel won the title in 1988 and 1989 on the Honda RVF 750 RC 30. This had a power output of 140 hp (103 kW) at 13,500 rpm. In most of the following years, however, the two-cylinder Ducatis were able

to take advantage of their larger engine size and convert it into wins and titles.

It was not until 1997 that the situation changed in favor of Honda. The American John Kocinski won the title after 24 races with a clear lead over British rider Carl Fogerty on a Ducati. To regain the initiative, the Chief Engineer at Honda Racing, Suhei Nakamoto, had to achieve an explosion in power output. Thanks to his efforts, the four-cycle V4 RVF 750 RC 45 with an included angle of 90 degrees and short-stroke geometry (bore 72 mm, stroke 46 mm) achieved 180 hp (132 kW) at 14,750 rpm – at the gearbox output, as Nakamoto was quick to point out. Mixture preparation was performed, very much in tune with the times, by an electronic fuel injection system which, like most of Honda's racing components, was developed in-house. The smooth power delivery and astonishingly good handling of this Honda superbike are attributed to the quality of this fuel supply system, in marked contrast to the situation 30 years ago, when the 499 cc Honda RC181 developed 90 hp (66 kW) – half as much power – and had the reputation of being too much of a handfull for fast riding. Those in the know are already saying that the superbikes of today will be the grand-prix machines of tomorrow. After all, when there are no more road bikes with two-cycle engines, World Championship battles can't be fought out with yesterday's technology – even if they promise to provide more power.

SMALL IS SMART AND SPEEDY

NOBUHIKO KAWAMOTO IS THE MAN WHO COMPLETED SOICHIRO HONDA'S WORK. HE JOINED HONDA IN 1960 WHEN HE LEFT UNIVERSITY. FROM 1963 ON, HONDA'S RACING DEPARTMENT WAS THE HARD SCHOOL IN WHICH THE YOUNG ENGINEER STROVE FOR SUCCESS. HIS MASTERPIECE: THE ARCHITECTURE OF THE FORMULA 1 ENGINES. SOON WORLD CHAMPIONSHIP TITLES WERE THE REWARD, AND KAWAMOTO BECAME HEAD OF TECHNICAL DEVELOPMENT. IN 1992 HE SUCCEEDED TO THE LEGACY OF SOICHIRO HONDA HIMSELF AND BECAME DIRECTOR OF THE WORLDWIDE GROUP OF COMPANIES BEARING THIS PROUD NAME.

SMALL IS SMART AND SPEEDY

Nobuhiko Kawamoto

First evidence seems to suggest that Nobu-hiko Kawamoto had a typically Japanese career at Honda. He joined the company in 1960 as a racing mechanic and rose to be chief executive before handing over to Hiroyuki Yoshino in 1998. The facts do not bear this out, however: throughout his career, Kawamoto was a manager far removed from the conventional Japanese image. He acquired most of his style of leadership from the brilliant Soichiro Honda himself, and directed the company in a success-oriented sporting spirit, almost as if were a single gigantic racing team. Clauspeter Becker was able to conduct various conversations with his friend Nobuhiko Kawamoto in Japan and in Europe.

What form did your engineer's training take?
Kawamoto: My father was professor of bio-logy at a state-run university, and earned very little money in the post-war years. There was no question of my going to an expensive private university. I applied for a grant and went to a state-run college of advanced technology.

Were you involved with motor vehicles right from the start?
Kawamoto: I certainly was! I bought myself a 250 cc Pointer motorcycle. I couldn't afford a Honda ...!

You had enough money for that?
Kawamoto: Of course – I spent my grant on it!

How did the Pointer perform?
Kawamoto: Not very well and not very often, so that I soon made the acquaintance of the man who ran the university's workshop. Whenever we students wanted to repair something we invited him for a drink and then we not only had the run of the workshop but the benefit of his practical experience too.

So it wasn't a great disadvantage for you to have to attend this university?
Kawamoto: When I look back – no. I learned a lot of useful practical things there too. To improve the cash situation, we students used to patch up old pre-war cars. If the weather was good we worked outside – we even dug ourselves an inspection pit inside the university grounds!

What kind of cars were they?
Kawamoto: Many of them were old American models. I well remember the first one, a Buick with a vast eight-cylinder engine. It took twenty of my fellow-students to lift the cylinder head off.

I guess you enjoyed doing all this.
Kawamoto: Sure, but I probably wasted too much time that way.

Did you ever get to hear any lectures?
Kawamoto: Not many! I doubt if people today would call it a proper course of study. But even then, the practical training in industry was excellent.

Which company took you on?
Kawamoto: Yamaha, of all people!

SMALL IS SMART AND SPEEDY

In 1964, when the Honda RA 272 Fomula 1 racing car took its first tentative steps to fame, Kawamoto was employed in the company's competition department

What happened after that?

Kawamoto: A professor suggested applying for a job with Toyota.

But nothing came of it?

Kawamoto: No, because I wanted to go to Honda.

When did you start there?

Kawamoto: In 1963. Kiyoshi Kawashima took me on personally.

Why did you have this determination to work for Honda?

Kawamoto: Because I was so enthusiastic about its world championship motorcycle team.

Were you already an admirer of Soichiro Honda?

Kawamoto: Not as much as I am today. I was more interested in the racing. Today I'm full of respect when I look back on how he pro-

gressed from a manufacturer of motorized bicycles to the winning team in the Formula 1 world championship.

What was your first meeting with Soichiro Honda like?

Kawamoto: As you can imagine, it was a sobering experience. He welcomed us young engineers with the words: 'Everything you know is theory, therefore you don't know anything! Everything you need to know you will have to learn here!'

And is that how it happened?

Kawamoto: Certainly. I was lucky to be chosen from 14 applicants to join the racing department. I don't know how I survived my first outing with them: the Brabham Formula 2 car, making its first appearance, failed to leave the starting line – I'd installed the wrong clutch!

So you were a racing mechanic?

Kawamoto: Correct, though they used to call us racing engineers because it sounded more important.

How did Soichiro Honda react to such a disastrous blunder?

Kawamoto: He was mighty angry.

But that wasn't the end of your career in the racing department?

Kawamoto: No, because of Soichiro Honda's principle that since all men are individuals, they're bound to make mistakes.

Have you adopted the same attitude?

Kawamoto: Yes I have, because I see it as one of my tasks to maintain the managerial culture of the man who founded our company.

Do you regard yourself as Soichiro Honda's successor?

Kawamoto: No – there was only one Honda. He was a genius, and he taught us that we can only achieve something great if we have confidence in ourselves.

Was this the key to those later successes in Formula 2?

Kawamoto: In theory yes, but not in practice. We owe almost everything we achieved then to Jack Brabham. He taught us how to succeed in motor racing. It's an honor for us that we have been able to benefit from his services as an advisor.

I believe you did leave Honda for a short time.

Kawamoto: Yes, that was in 1968, when the racing department was closed. I flew to London – with the Russian Aeroflot airline, because it was cheaper. I wanted to join Cosworth in England, and Keith Duckworth did in fact offer me a job.

But Cosworth was only a short interlude?

Kawamoto: Yes, because Director Tadashi Kume told me that Honda wouldn't stay out of motor racing for ever and that in any case this was only a small aspect of the complete task.

What happened then?

Kawamoto: Together with Kume I worked on two sports car projects, the Honda S 1000 and S 2000. They were both to have four-cylinder engines with four-valve combustion chambers, plenty of power and an engine speed limit of 7,000 revs. There was even a plan to use these engines in boats and sports aircraft. The first S 1000 prototypes were very promising: they performed better than the Lotus Elite.

But something went wrong?

Kawamoto: Soichiro Honda demanded that we should use air-cooled engines. He felt that if they worked for VW they would work for Honda too.

That was the start of the adventure with the air-cooled Formula 1 V8 engine?

Kawamoto: That wasn't everything: we also developed the Honda 1300 passenger car with a transverse air-cooled engine at the front. It was thermally unstable in a big way and ran so hot that the paint on the hood was discolored. It was a nightmare!

Your career at Honda has been divided into three main phases: first of all you were racing engineer, then technical director and finally Chief

SMALL IS SMART AND SPEEDY

Exercutive of Honda Motors. What experience did you take with you from one phase to the next?

Kawamoto: My philosophy of work has always been to plan for the next dimension from whatever position I find myself in. When I was racing engineer I always thought hard about the plans I would push ahead with when I became head of development. And when I was given that job I tended to think ahead to what I would do if I ever became Managing Director.

When you took on this job, what did you think about then?

Kawamoto: I guess I sometimes find myself thinking about how I would govern Japan!

Does that mean we can look forward to Prime Minister Kawamoto some time soon?

Kawamoto (laughs loudly): Oh no, I've decided that politics is the wrong business for me. It will certainly be better for me and for the company if I think instead about passing on my experience to the next generation of managers and the one that follows it.

What message would you like to pass on to the next generation?

Kawamoto: That we need clearly defined objectives and reliable leadership. Every employee has to be prepared to accept full responsibility. And above all, Honda needs a strong Chief Executive – a constant reincarnation of Soichiro Honda.

Since Yoshino took over as Chief Executive, you officially have the status of an advisor. In the current situation, what advice would you give to a Japanese company?

Kawamoto: I think it's very important for Japan to be well represented and for the self-confidence of the Japanese to be strengthened. There is no point in lamenting over defeat in the Second World War and worrying whether we can survive in the current climate of competition.

After 50 successful years, the risk for Honda is surely very small?

Kawamoto: We must nevertheless consolidate our identity and communicate our corporate culture even more clearly. I say this because I believe we are entitled to be proud of our position as an international corporation that has never lost its fundamental Japanese qualities. Even as a global player, we have never become European or American.

How do you see Honda's position in relation to international competition?

Kawamoto: I still see Honda as a young company that has a lot to learn. Fifty years are only a short period compared with the long tradition of the Europeans. We must therefore continue to learn and abide by the basic principle laid down by Soichiro Honda: in a large company it's always much easier to teach than to learn.

What are Honda's shortcomings?

Kawamoto: I think I would prefer to start with the strong points. We are in a good position on the American market these days, but Europe is much farther away that America for us. Thanks to our cooperation with Rover, we understand the British best. The multicultural society on the continent of Europe is

Kawamoto started his career at Honda as a "racing engineer". His comment: "In actual fact I was a mechanic in the racing team"

something we must learn to understand much better.

Mr. Kawamoto, you once said that a "world car" is nonsense and that cars should be built to suit the markets in the countries in which they are sold. What proportion ought to be built according to this principle?

Kawamoto: It should relate to at least 60 percent of total output, with under 40 percent remaining standardized. This is a trend that still offers scope for improvement, particularly in Germany, where the customers are exceptionally critical.

What needs to be done?

Kawamoto: The Japanese must understand the need to live like Europeans if they are genuinely to understand them

What impresses you about Europe?

Kawamoto: I have great respect for the confidence with which European engineers master their tasks; it's something that comes from their long experience.

In the nineteen-eighties you spoke about Mercedes-Benz with great respect. How do you see the company today?

Kawamoto: Some of its models caused me to have doubts. But the determined way in which the weak points were eliminated shows me how rapidly and effectively the people at Mercedes learn their lessons.

What do you think of the A- Class and the Smart in this connection?

Kawamoto: Both of them tell me that Mercedes is still on a learning curve – but this is no problem for good management.

Which European manager impresses you in particular?

Kawamoto: Dr. Ferdinand Piëch. I met him here in Japan some years ago, when he was still at Audi. As that company's chief executive, he was personally looking into the question of how an Audi ought to be built for the Japanese market. To do that, he immersed himself systematically in Japanese culture.

What are Piëch's special features today, as head of the complete VW Group?

Kawamoto: He is a combination of talented engineer and convincing manager – there aren't many people like him.

Just the two of you, perhaps?

Kawamoto (acknowledges the compliment with a smile): No, I can think of three!

Who's the third one?

Kawamoto: Lutz.

But Robert Lutz is a visionary, not an engineer.

Kawamoto: Even so, he made sure that Chrysler built the right kind of car.

He was opposed to the merger with Daimler-Benz.

Kawamoto: I think he was expressing his personal conviction there, instead of the urge for greater size and higher profits.

Do the current Honda models all confirm Kawamoto's view that high-grade technical features are an unmistakable Honda trade mark – even the baby Logo, for instance, with its beam axle at the rear?

Kawamoto: Although the Japanese economic situation is difficult, Honda's strategy is to boost its worldwide production from two

SMALL IS SMART AND SPEEDY

*Nobuhiko Kawamoto:
"We want to build and
sell fuel-cell vehicles
from 2003 on. In view
of the progress we have
already made, this
shouldn't present any
problems"*

and half to three million annually. We can't achieve this volume only with expensive, high-class cars at the moment. We have to make a few technical and price concessions.

The new S 2000 Roadster isn't dramatically different from its competitors and seems to have abandoned the policy we saw in the S 600 thirty-five years ago, that Honda's sports cars ought to have unmistakable technical features.

Kawamoto: I would have liked to give the Roadster a two-liter V8 engine, but I had to listen when people told me that times have changed. Young people today expect the marketing experts to give them a realistic car that they can enjoy without breaking the bank. We chose the four-cylinder engine because we are a big corporation and a market-niche model would have been too risky.

Should this prove to be wrong, then I have already threatened to come back and re-introduce some of the old technical ideas!

Honda's "Small ist Smart" slogan dates from your period as Chief Executive. Is it still valid?

Kawamoto: Absolutely, in fact I'd like to add to it and say: "Small is Smart and Speedy".

In earlier years Honda confirmed its advanced technological approach more often by exhibiting unusual cars. Today the company's progress seems to be demonstrated by prototype aircraft or robots instead.

Kawamoto: Developing a humanoid robot was a big challenge for our engineers. This is the kind of task from which one learns a lot. But Honda's view is that we shall need robots like this in the future. If the current population trend continues, Japan will only have 60 million inhabitants in 100 years' time, about half as many as today. We shall have too few people prepared to perform the unpleasant tasks that nobody likes doing. Robots may then be the only solution. Nor should we forget that less than 30 percent of the surface of the earth can be reached by wheeled vehicles. If the robots help us to teach machines to "walk on their own feet", our mobility will be improved. If the world needs robots, they will be an interesting alternative for a company such as Honda if sales of automobiles should show a permanent tendency to decrease.

In other words, Honda's development perspectives look well ahead into the future?
Kawamoto: This is a traditional strategy for us. We have always pursued forward-looking policies, even if we have not put all of them into production. For instance, a Honda team has for some time now been developing an aircraft, including the turbine engines to power it, but there has so far been no decision on whether Honda should start to build aircraft at some future date.

When the economic situation is difficult, how can one justify such complex and expensive projects?
Kawamoto: Honda is fully convinced that this work is important and justifiable. In fact we have taken a further courageous step and started an entirely new department called HDF, which stands for Honda Development Future. It's a small organization that can operate entirely free from economic or other

constraints and work out alternative solutions to various problems.

That brings us to alternative vehicle propulsion systems. Which direction do you think that developments will take?
Kawamoto: At Honda, we favor the fuel cell. We want to market fuel-cell vehicles from 2003 onwards. According to the situation at present, we should easily be able to keep to this schedule. We shall see!

Does this mean that all the current projects such as the Zero Level Emission Vehicle, the electric car or the hybrid power train are only temporary solutions?
Kawamoto: That is correct. We regard these concepts as bridges leading to the fuel-cell vehicle.

Japan, North America and Europe will certainly be capable in the future of organizing their road trsaffic on environmentally acceptable lines. But what about China and the many threshold countries that are only just entering the motorized transport era?
Kawamoto: Honda will establish itself in China in the coming years, not only with production plants and motor vehicles but also by arousing a sense of social responsibility. If we succeed in this, it may be possible to build up the necessary infrastructure for environmentally acceptable cars and supply them with unleaded gasoline. Honda certainly intends to build cars soon for China that comply with the American emission limits.

Is that economically viable for China?
Kawamoto: In China, cars are only bought by

106

prosperous people who are prepared to pay a higher price for a modern car.

Elsewhere, prosperous people always tend to buy larger cars that use more fuel and are ecologically objectionable: luxury cars with twelve or possibly even more cylinders, increasingly gigantic off-roaders and more and more "power pickups", at least in the USA.

Kawamoto: The car industry should extend the lower and not the upper end of its model program.

Kawamotosan, you have given us a glimpse of a future in which a lot may change, possibly everything. What ought not to be allowed to change?

Kawamoto: Honda. It must remain Honda!

The first one sees of a new car are sketches: this is the sports study model 01 dating from 1997

INTERNATIONAL SUCCESS

I N THE EARLY 1960S, SOICHIRO HONDA HAD FOUGHT THE GOVERNMENT'S INTENTION TO PRE-VENT HIS RAPIDLY EXPANDING COM-PANY (WHICH WAS EARNING GOOD MONEY) FROM STARTING TO BUILD AUTOMOBILES.
AS WAS TO BE EXPECTED, HONDA TOOK UP THE FIGHT SUCCESSFULLY FOR THE FREE-MARKET ECONOMY AGAINST THIS EXCESSIVE DEGREE OF STATE INFLUENCE WITH A NUMBER OF UNUSUAL PUBLIC RELATIONS CAMPAIGNS. BY PRESENTING HIS T 360 AND S 360 MODELS TO THE PUBLIC, HE CONFRONTED THE AUTHORITIES WITH A SITUATION IN WHICH THEY WERE FORCED TO GIVE WAY.

In the fall of 1962 the Honda S 360 Cabriolet was the sensation of the Tokyo Motor Show – its small four-cylinder engine developed a remarkable 33 horsepower at 900 rpm

People began to gather and admire the small sports car wherever it was exhibited

Honda's action labeled the company as 'atypical' in the eyes of the politicians, simply because it wasn't easy to influence. Deliveries of the first Honda cars began in the spring of 1963, and in the first year the modest total of 136 found their way onto the road. As well as the S 360 shown to the public in the fall of the previous year, there was now an S 500. The letter S stood for 'Sport', and both cars shared the same body: a small two-seater convertible with a correspondingly small but free-revving engine. The result was a kind of performance that had never before been available in this category. The S 360's 354-cc water-cooled four-cylinder engine developed 33 horsepower at a remarkable 9,000 rpm; the 492-cc unit for the S 500 had an output of 40 hp at 8,000 rpm. The top speeds were of the order of 120 and 130 km/h (75 and 81 mph) respectively, and with independent suspension all round, the roadhold-

110

In August 1963 Honda began to build the T 360, which was given an enthusiastic reception

ing was satisfactory too. Enthusiastic drivers were even able to order a five-speed gearbox instead of the usual four-speed unit, and in that way to keep the little light-alloy four-cylinder engine with its overhead camshaft turning over at the high speeds for which it was designed.

Japanese drivers' hearts went out to these baby sports cars immediately. Whereas other manufacturers were still producing cars designed mainly to carry their occupants in relative comfort from place to place, Honda had once again detected what the public actually wanted and was now ready for: a small sports car priced at a level that many people could afford, with good looks and plenty of performance. For export markets a more powerful S 600 version was rapidly put together, with a 575-cc engine developing 57 horsepower and a top speed of 145 km/h (90 mph).

In 1965 these cars, with many features that the European market found unusual, were seen in Germany for the first time: they took part in a race on the Nürburg Ring circuit and carried off the 1000-cc class victory with ease. The winning car was driven by someone who was later to have a most successful career in touring car racing: Hubert Hahne.

It was not until October 1966 that the Honda name was added to the list of automobile manufacturers selling their cars in Europe.

This was the month in which the S 800 was exhibited at the Paris Motor Show as a coupe and a convertible. The small sports car once again captivated enthusiasts from the very start, the car magazines looked closely at its unusual technical specification but could find

Before long the S 600 Cabriolet, which appeared in March 1964, was joined by an attractive Coupe

111

INTERNATIONAL SUCCESS

The S 800 not only amazed the automobile experts but also captured the hearts of young customers who had waited a long time for such an agile baby roadster

nothing to criticize and the dealers looked forward to the start of sales. Now with a 791-cc engine, Japan's popular sports car went on sale in Europe with an output of 67 horsepower, enough to provoke the magazine auto, motor und sport into writing that "the Japanese evidently have a distinct lead in the building of high-performance engines". Journalist Gerd Hack went on: "The outward appearance of this two-seater sports car contains very few clues to its country of origin. Its styling is individual but not unconventional. But open the hood and you discover that the Far Eastern designers know how to appeal to car fans and frighten their market rivals. The Honda shows us what modern, state-of-the-art engine design can achieve: it has a water-cooled four-cylinder unit with double overhead camshafts, but there the resemblance to everyday power units ends. The remarkable thing about this engine is not its basic construction principle but the skill and ingenuity that has gone into it."

The article continued: "To mobilize 67 horsepower one normally needs an engine size of about one and a half liters. Honda gets this power from just under 800 cubic centimeters, an output per liter of 85 horsepower – the kind of figure one would expect from a racing car!" The magazine summed up: "All in all, one can't help coming to the conclusion that the Japanese have a distinct lead in the building of high-performance engines." The Honda S 800 went on sale as a coupe or convertible, the same price (at the time, 7,750 Marks in Germany) being charged for both versions of this highly unusual baby sports car.

Before sales could start, however, the Honda head offices in Hamburg had to build up a dealer network. Wolfgang Murrmann, one of the pioneers, recalls: "Sales in Germany started in 1967 with the S 800. A year before this we began to develop a strategy that would lead to the build-up of a dealer organization. We wrote to no fewer than ten thousand car dealers and offered them our products. The response rate wasn't very high, but at least we ended up with 300 names on our list."

The next move was very unusual: "We set up a mobile exhibition and took it on tour through Germany. In the largest towns and cities we hired a large hall and showed our motorbikes and cars initially to the dealers we had invited, later to the general public.

The small 0.8-liter four-cylinder engine with a separate carburetor for each cylinder developed 67 hp and was admired by technical people all over the world

INTERNATIONAL SUCCESS

If Soichiro Honda was asked where he liked working most of all he would reply: "In the engine development department!" This was where, with his young team of engineers, he could develop a series of fresh ideas and concepts

These were purely and simply information events: we made no effort to sell the vehicles because this would have competed with the existing Honda dealers. The response to this campaign was encouraging: as a result of the tour 80 new dealer contracts were signed.

After this major exploration of the German market Honda could call upon the services of about 200 dealers, and the head offices of European Honda Motor Trading Co. in Hamburg rapidly became too small. Here was also a threat from another side: the company had originally been set up to pioneer sales in Europe, but in the meantime there were separate European Honda subsidiaries that were taking over many of its responsibilities. There was only conclusion to be drawn from

this: the trading company was wound up and a 'genuine' German subsidiary established to take its place: Honda Deutschland GmbH. A suitable location was found in Offenbach, in the Frankfurt area, and a new start was made in the spring of 1968 with 30 employees who expressed their willingness to move from Hamburg. Prospects for the new company were bright: following 454 Honda car registrations in 1967 (about 70 percent of them for the S 800, the remainder for the just-launched N 600), the figure rose to 1,947 by the end of 1968 – encouraging growth that must have been welcomed by the parent company in Tokyo.

Activities of this kind took Honda farther down the road toward the status of a global corporation. Even after his first visits to the USA and Europe, Soichiro Honda had been convinced that a company could only grow steadily if it were active on a global scale. He began to put his motto into effect at a very early stage: 'Think global, act local'. The idea behind this was self-evident: to study and satisfy the wishes of people wherever they happened to live and to supply products positioned on local markets in a way that would appeal to these people.

The story of how and with what speed Honda founded subsidiary companies all over the world has been told elsewhere. The American Honda Motor Company Inc., established in 1959, was to prove the most important of all these subsidiaries, since it had the task of cre-

ating the company's largest and most important market. Today, about a million vehicles are sold annually in the USA, which thus absorbs more Honda automobiles than Japan itself or Europe. On the European continent, Germany and Great Britain head the registration charts with annual sales of about 60,000 vehicles in each case.

Such figures were surely undreamed of by the managers back in Japan when they introduced the N 600 small car. Originally shown to the public in March 1967 as the N 360, and powered by a small air-cooled twin-cylinder engine, it was an immediate hit. Within two months, Honda had sold 5,570 cars and secured 31.2 percent of this market segment. By the end of the first year, sales were running at 20,000 cars a month. A year later Honda was able to announce that it had broken every record in this segment of the automobile market. A station wagon and a small delivery van were rapidly developed on the basis of the N 360, and in no time at all Honda had another two best-sellers on its

hands. Not surprisingly, its management came to the conclusion that a larger-engined version of this model would sell successfully on export markets too. The 42-hp twin-cylinder car was therefore offered for sale in Europe, with either a four-speed manual-shift gearbox or the company's 'Hondamatic' three-speed automatic transmission. Although the list price was impressively low (4,894 Marks on the German market), the car nevertheless sold sluggishly and in Germany in particular aroused very little interest among potential customers. It was simply too small for its day, and conditions in the hectic traffic of Tokyo were too different from the less congested roads of Germany and in particular its inter-city 'autobahn' highways.

Shortly after this, the parent company back in Japan itself ran into difficulties of an entirely technical nature: the first 'large' Honda automobile, the Honda 1300, was announced in October 1968. Soichiro Honda had decided to concentrate on performance, and had given it a 1.3-liter, four-cylinder engine devel-

The N 360, introduced in 1967, had an air-cooled 354 cc engine with a maximum output of 31 horsepower at 8500 rpm

115

Soichiro Honda and his close friend and associate Takeo Fujisawa (right) at the Third Honda Idea Contest, held in September 1972 in Hamamatsu – just a year before both of them retired from the company

oping 100 horsepower. The 1300 had a top speed of 175 km/h (109 mph) – but Honda had also insisted that the engine should be air-cooled. He joined his engineering staff in the struggle to eliminate the shortcomings of this engine concept: "The outcome of this period of intensive thinking and testing was an air cooling system that we named DDAC (Duo-Dyna-Air-Cooling). It prevented engine overheating, eliminated the noise problems otherwise associated with air cooling and enabled us to extract 100 horsepower without difficulty from the 1.3-liter engine."

There are still Honda employees who rate the 1300 model very highly, but with hindsight one can see that the designers in Hamamatsu failed to come up with the car that the public wanted. Soichiro Honda's own view: "I

believe that the car's elegant styling ought to have made it a best-seller – but our customers wanted something different." Other Honda engineers put the blame less on the car's appearance than on its technical specification, which they felt to be too sporty in character. Dry sump lubrication, engine speeds of more than 8,000 rpm and the noise of an air-cooled four-cylinder engine, they felt, were out of place in a midsize family car. Fujisawa also praised the 1300's performance, but regretted that such advanced engineering was so expensive to build. Honda's comment in his memoirs sounds a note of genuine surprise: "According to him (Fujisawa), our company was subsidizing every car we sold!"

Initially, Honda's view prevailed: if the 1300 had teething troubles, they could be eliminated. This was the time in which the US government introduced new clauses to the country's 'Clean Air Act' and called for further reductions in vehicle exhaust emissions, to a level never attempted by the industry before. By 1975 no new cars were to be licensed unless their hydrocarbon and carbon monoxide emissions were some 90 percent lower than before. A year later the level of oxides of nitrogen was also to be cut in the same drastic way. It was evident that Honda's high-revving engines would be at a disadvantage – but the company's chief executive remained loyal to the air-cooled engine and declared that with sufficient research even this problem would be solved.

The mood within the company rapidly sank to a new low point. On one side the chief executive, Honda himself, was determined to pursue his chosen policy; on the other the engineers in the research and development departments had performed innumerable tests and knew only too well that the forthcoming emission limits could only be met by a water-cooled engine.

Fujisawa, Honda's friend and co-founder of the company, the man without whose efforts it could well have ceased to exist, found himself in the middle, between these two diametrically opposed viewpoints. He summoned the responsible engineers to a conference which Soichiro Honda was not asked to attend. The engineers were able to convince the company's Number Two executive that in only a few years' time Honda would be unable to comply with the new automobile licensing laws and that it would have to work long and hard to do so with a range of new water-cooled engines.

Let us see how Honda himself takes up the story: "After that secret meeting Fujisawa called on me and invited me for a meal. I was surprised, because we hadn't seen each other at all for some time. He must have something important on his mind, I thought, as I sat beside him in his car. On the one hand I was pleased to see him again, but on the other hand his stern expression began to worry me. When we were sitting at our table in the restaurant, he began to speak in an almost excited tone of voice, and told me every detail of the conference he had just held. I replied that my air cooling system would also be perfectly capable of satisfying the new exhaust emission limits. His response made me go rigid with horror: I should decide whether I wanted to remain President of the corporation or go back to working on my project as an engineer!"

The decision is now well-known: Soichiro Honda remained in office as President, his engineers were allowed to pursue the policy they considered correct – and the company's success story continued.

Honda seems to have accepted the consequences of this 'palace revolution' without bad feeling: "In fact I was soon able to convince myself of the advantages of the water-cooled engine. I was glad that the engineers who I had trained and who had supported me for so long were now so advanced in their research work that they were able to surpass my own efforts. My goal was achieved and my wishes more than fulfilled when they took over from me. What could have been an unpleasant moment in my life was thus transformed into a time of great happiness."

The first prototype featuring the new engine was built in the fall of 1969, and within two years Honda was able to surprise the public with its CVCC (Compound Vortex Controlled

*The first Honda auto-
mobiles – these are the
N 360 of 1967 and the
L 700 of 1965 – still
had engines closely
based on motorcycle
designs*

Combustion) system. It was used on the first
engine capable of fulfilling the 1975 US
exhaust emission regulations without an
additional catalytic converter. This was a
major step forward, with Honda showing the
world the direction that passenger-car engine
design would have to take. The CVCC system
was a source of considerable embarrassment
to other manufacturers: the US companies,
for instance, were planning to protest against
the government's emission control legisla-
tion in order to gain an additional year before the new limits came into force. Japanese manufacturers too were prepared to support this protest but now Honda had shown
with its new system that the solution was
already available! It needed several years of
further development work, of course, before
the CVCC principle was ready for series production, but Honda's name was suddenly in
the public eye.

Before all this, in June 1971, the 'Life' small
car was announced – conclusive evidence that
the air-cooled engine adventure was coming
to an end. This small car, with a 356-cc inline twin-cylinder engine developing 30 hp at
a typically high engine speed of 8,000 rpm,
weighed only 490 kilograms (1,080 lbs) and
had a top speed of just under 110 km/h
(68 mph). A more sporty version followed
soon, with an output of 36 hp at 9,000 rpm.
For this car, with its top speed of 120 km/h
(75 mph), a five-speed gearbox was available. In Japan, the Life also appeared as a

*The 1300, the last Honda
model, with a 100 hp air-
cooled engine: available
as a Coupe and sedan,
customers found it too
sporty*

station wagon, but Europe did not see this version. Instead, it began to look forward to the appearance of the Honda Civic, which had its world premiere in July 1972.

This new model, soon to enjoy impressive international sales success, represented a departure once for all from the earlier Honda policy that the engine's power output was all that mattered. A compact two-door car, it was sensible and well-balanced in its design with practical dimensions and plenty of space inside. Its inline four-cylinder engine for the first time didn't depend on exotic speeds for its peak power output, but developed it at the normal speed of 5,500 rpm.

Honda, it would seem, had once again understood what the near future would need: a practical, economical midsize car that its dealers were able to sell like hot cakes during and after the first international oil crisis. Just as Honda himself had recognized that his countrymen needed mobility in the aftermath of the Second World War, and satisfied this demand with motorized bicycles and motorcycles, so his company now had these small, sporty cars that were an attractive alternative for those who didn't fancy a boring, conventional sedan but had no money for a sports car.

At the beginning of 1973 Fujisawa informed a surprised administrative board that he proposed to retire. He took this decision quite alone and told no-one in advance. Soichiro

Honda reacted at once, as his memoirs tell us: "We began our task together, and therefore we had to lay it down together. Fujisawa, who had not been aware of the high esteem in which I held him, was deeply moved by my decision."

And so the founder of the Honda company and his second-in-command retired at the same time, 25 years after they had begun their work together. "We met again soon afterwards, but our conversation consisted entirely of our thanking each other! It was one of the shortest conversations we ever had. 'We went through a lot of ups and downs together, didn't we?' 'But it was a very pleasant time.' 'My life was very enjoyable too, and I'm grateful to you!' It doesn't matter who said what, we spoke as a single voice. The word 'pleasant' said everything, and there was nothing more for me to add. My vice-president had given me the best possible opportunity of retiring …"

This step was taken officially in October 1973, but both the company's founders

The Life sedan of 1971 was the first Honda car to have a water-cooled four-cylinder engine, in this case a 356 cc, 30 hp unit. The sporty Z Coupe of 1970, on the other hand, was still powered by a 31 hp air-cooled engine

In March 1973 Honda presented its contribution to the "safety car" topic, based on the Civic CVCC with its extremely low-emission engine

Starting in 1964, Honda France had its offices not far from the celebrated Crazy Horse Saloon – From 1972 on, the Civic achieved sales success all over the world. The first model was rated at 60 bhp and had a top speed of 145 km/h (90 mph)

remained non-executive directors and advisers for a while after, though without the right to act or speak on behalf of the company. Fujisawa was 62 years old at the time, Honda himself 66.

Even though it now lacked the direct influence of those who had guided its fortunes for so long, the company nevertheless prospered mightily. All over the world, further subsidiaries and production companies were set up and adopted a policy of tying in closely with the national cultures of the countries

in which they were situated. When asked for instance why Honda France S.A. had its head offices in the immediate neighborhood of the Crazy Horse Saloon in Paris, Soichiro Honda replied "Because of a desire to concern ourselves with the culture of the host country!"

The Civic was just the car the market had been waiting for, and became a best-seller in no time at all. It looked like a 'real car' and its concept was a sensible one: four-cylinder inline engine installed transversely at the front and front-wheel drive to provide as much interior space as possible. Weight-saving design mean that the 60 horsepower obtained from the 1.2-liter engine only had to propel 600 to 650 kilograms (1,320 to 1435 lbs) of body weight, depending on the car's equipment. Not surprisingly, performance was lively, with a top speed of 145 km/h (90 mph) and a time of only 12.8 seconds from a standing start to 100 km/h (62 mph).

Sales of the Honda Civic in Germany began in the summer of 1974, and before long the country's Honda subsidiary was able to report record turnover: 82,333,000 German Marks (DM) in the 1974/75 fiscal year, for instance, with 8,216,000 DM accounted for by the cars. The Civic had made Honda popular again – but it was not until the Accord model line appeared that sales on export markets really took off.

The Civic was soon introduced in station-wagon guise, badged as the Van

This was the photo with which Honda Deutschland introduced the first-generation Civic to the German market

The Accord was launched in May 1976. It was an elegant sedan with a 1.6-liter, 80-horsepower engine – the next, logical step toward a program that would also include larger models. Although the Accord's body didn't seem particularly large, it proved to have an enormous amount of space inside. Even tall Americans felt happy inside it (though if they wanted to take their surfboard down to the coast with them, they were obliged to put it on the roof rack). The Accord Hatchback, as the name implies, was the answer to even this minor problem (the Civic was now available in a hatchback body style as well), and the rear seat could be folded down if necessary to make the load area even larger. At the same time as the Accord, incidentally, a four-door version of the Civic was also introduced.

In car magazine articles, both models were much praised. The German periodical 'auto, motor und sport' wrote for instance in December 1980 about the Civic 1300 SL: "It's well-balanced qualities make the Honda Civic an attractive offer, if not a particularly low-priced one. It costs more or less what would be charged for a rival German prod-

The four-door Accord first reached dealers' showrooms in October 1977 – and also became a best-seller in a very short time

uct, but for this money it not only has four doors but also the kind of full equipment list we have come to expect from the Japanese." With its 60-hp engine the Civic had a top speed of 147.5 km/h (91.7 mph) and needed 14.6 seconds for the sprint from 0 to 100 km/h (62 mph). Its fuel consumption during the magazine's test was 9.3 liters per 100 kilometers (25.3 US mpg), and the journalists summed up its advantages as "reasonable interior space, full equipment specification, low fuel consumption and good road behaviour". The shortcomings were listed as "small trunk, skimpy seats, high noise level and limited suspension comfort".
What was the final verdict on this occasion?

"The Accord, compared with its Japanese rivals, is easily the most attractive looking car in its class. Honda's models had a European look when their local competitors were still heavily under the influence of baroque American styling. Honda, the world's largest motorcycle manufacturer, shows us that it also sets the standards in Japanese automobile engineering."

The Accord, launched in its original form in May 1976, with the four-door sedan following in October 1977, was joined later, in November 1978, by the Prelude Coupe, which was not a pure two-seater but a 2+2 model, since as the press release declared

'even the most sporty driver sometimes has some luggage with him'. The 1,6- (80-hp) or 1.8-liter (90-hp) four-cylinder engines were good for a top speed of between 155 and 165 km/h (96 and 103 mph).

Sales success, however, was limited. The German magazine mot put this down less to any technological shortcomings than to the 'still rather baroque styling'. When the next Prelude appeared in November 1982, this supposed drawback had been radically eliminated. The new Prelude was described as 'elegant and powerful' by the auto-zeitung, and mot described the technical details of the latest Prelude in the following terms: "The 1.8-liter four-cylinder engine is available with two power outputs: 105 hp (77 kW) with a manual-shift gearbox and 100 hp (74 kW) with automatic. A notable feature of these transverse engines is that they have three valves per cylinder, two inlet and one exhaust. Such a technical novelty arouses interest, and the three-valve cylinder head is alleged to ensure an especially good fuel-air mixture and improve the combustion process."

A test carried out by the auto-zeitung did indeed confirm that Honda's technicians were on the right track with their twelve-valve cylinder head. The journalists wrote: "One hundred horsepower whisk this elegant coupe up to 100 km/h (62 mph) in 11.2 seconds. The torque curve is an indication that four additional inlet valves are at work here."

The remainder of the test was also largely positive in tone: "All in all, the Prelude's chassis and suspension were also positive aspects of its design. The Honda Prelude EX with catalytic converter is a bargain for those who wish to protect the environment – and for music lovers too, since a Blaupunkt radio with cassette player is included in the price!"

The next Accord (or Vigor, as it was called on some export markets) appeared in September 1981 and was also much admired. It was once again larger in its overall dimensions than before, and retained the four-cylinder 1.6- and 1.8-liter engines from the previous model. Two body styles were offered: a two-door hatchback and a four-door sedan. The prices, unfortunately, went up in parallel with the size of the car: Honda asked about eight percent more for its new Accord, which had a severely negative effect on sales volume.

This was the year in which cooperation with the British Austin Rover Group (still known as British Leyland at the time) began. Honda and British Leyland Ltd. had signed their first agreement on technical cooperation in December 1979, the aim being for Honda to develop a midsize car that would be built by Leyland.

There had been speculation about such cooperation earlier in the year. The German newspaper Süddeutsche Zeitung wrote on

INTERNATIONAL SUCCESS

Evolution instead of revolution – this certainly applied to the second Civic generation that was on sale from 1979 to 1983

April 4: "British Leyland Plans to Cooperate with Honda" and continued: "This would give the Japanese automobile industry a decisive means of penetrating the European market, at a time when the EC Commission is considering whether to impose restrictions on Japanese imports. The key element in this forthcoming cooperation will probably be the manufacture of a midsize Honda model under license, possibly the Accord. This would give Leyland a chance to bridge the gap before developing a similar model of its own for 1982/83."

Sure enough, on Dezember 28, 1979 the news agencies reported: "British Leyland to Build a Car for Honda." The following more detailed report stated: British Leyland Ltd. (BL) of London and the Honda Motor Corp. of Tokyo have signed an agreement to assem-

ble a Japanese car jointly in Great Britain. The Honda model Bounty (later called the Acclaim) is to be produced from 1981 on at the British Leyland plant in Cowley near Oxford. This will secure at least 3,000 jobs at the British company. By the mid-eighties up to 10,000 people should be employed directly or indirectly on this project. It is planned to produce about 90,000 cars a year."

The Acclaim was launched on October 7, 1981. It was developed from the Honda Ballade, itself a derivative of the Civic but with a wheelbase seven centimeters (2.8 inches) longer and a four-door body. The engine developed 70 horsepower and the car had a top speed of 154 km/h (95 mph) with manual-shift gearbox or 145 km/h (90 mph) with automatic. Even the British, who had lived with blanket speed limits for many years, found its performance rather modest, and the car was not destined to enjoy any great success.

Nevertheless, further agreements envisaging even closer cooperation were drawn up in later years, and as early as November 1981 it was decided to develop a further model as a joint project. The outcome in April 1984 was a contract with the Austin-Rover Group, as it had now become following the break-up of British Leyland. The new model eventually emerged as the Rover 213/216, and was also based on the new Acclaim.

The new Accord and the combined Honda-Leyland Acclaim project resulted in two new products appearing in 1981. They were joined in November by a new small car, the City. More than any other model, this car led to the Honda company's image changing rapidly, at least in Japan. It was the first evidence that a new generation of designers was at work. The City was small and agile, in other words just right for Japan's crowded urban streets. Its styling was so attractive that it soon collected one design award after another. With a generous window area and an astonishing amount of space inside, not to mention the two cheeky outside mirrors on the front fenders, it took the kids' fancy the moment it appeared. The press commented: "The City suddenly gave Honda a model that had no direct competitors. It was styled by a team with an average age of 26 – certainly far

more youthful than one would normally expect to find at work in Japan."

The Honda City had to undergo a change of name for Europe, where Opel had a prior claim to it. The City therefore became the 'Jazz'. The magazine auto-zeitung summed up the new small Honda, which was only 3.38 meters (133 inches) long as follows: "The styling may take some getting used to, but it certainly packs as much space as possible into a very small box – something that the highly stressed urban driver constantly searching for somewhere to park will value very highly. The suspension yields a comfortable ride, and whether on bumpy roads in the country or hustling along the German 'autobahn' the Honda Jazz always remains easy to control." The Jazz was propelled by a transverse inline four-cylinder engine with a dis-

In Japan the Honda City – sold in Europe as the Honda Jazz – was a big sales success. The European market, on the other hand, tended to regard it as too small

eration. Here the task was obvious: the Civic was Honda's top-volume car model and its purpose was therefore to bring the money in. Following the great success achieved by the City, the general public was naturally expecting the new Civic to be unusually good.

The covers came off in September 1983, when the German Motor Show (the 'IAA') in Frankfurt was chosen as the venue for the world premiere. Whereas the previous Civic had been sold as a two- or four-door sedan and as a station wagon, the new Civic line was more ambitious, and consisted of the two-door Civic, the four-door Civic Shuttle hatchback (a kind of leisure van that was joined just under eighteen months later by a version with four-wheel drive, the Civic Shuttle 4WD) and, last but not least, by a sensational small sports car, the CRX, with a 100-hp engine that held out the promise of excellent performance.

Whereas the sedan was fairly conservative in its styling, the Shuttle and the CRX were refreshingly new in appearance. Once again Honda had succeeded in interpreting the spirit of the times with great success. Had not the German car magazine auto, motor und sport already forecast in December of the previous year that a "small car would soon be acceptable in high society"? This was in an article headed "The Unusual Ideas with which the Japanese fill those Gaps in the Market". The implication behind the term 'high society'

Two cars that never went on sale in Europe; the Honda City Turbo and the amusing City Cabriolet

placement of 1,231 cc and a power output of 45 horsepower. Its top speed was measured by the testers as 135 km/h (82.5 mph), and it accelerated past the 100 km/h (62 mph) mark in 20.7 seconds.

A year after Honda's new start with its City model, it was the turn of the next Civic gen-

was not that Europe's remaining aristocrats would be able to influence the car market in some obscure way, but merely, as the magazine put it, that cars could well become higher off the ground, since this meant a more comfortable, relaxed seated position.

With 7,003 sales in Germany, the Shuttle admittedly only accounted for twelve percent of total Civic sales (60,109 even without the CRX), but "these were certainly customers who would have disregarded the Honda model program entirely had it not been for the Shuttle", as a company spokesman put it when the second-generation Shuttle was launched in March 1988. "We are confident that these customers won't want to be without this highly versatile leisure car in the future."

The Austrian magazine autorevue asummed up the Shuttle as follows: "Have you seen what it's like when a VW Bus falls in love with a Fiat Uno?" Later, the authors wrote in a rather more conciliatory tone: "It needs courage to be different. And it's a most welcome thing, because it opens up new perspectives and drives out boredom. At the moment the Japanese have a slight lead and the Europeans are tending to copy them. The Honda Civic is double confirmation of how things should go: first its styling and then its twelve-valve engine. We shall have to accustom ourselves more and more to shapes like this, which are not necessarily dedicated to

an ideal of beauty but make optimum use of every scrap of interior space."
A year later, when the Austrian magazine tested the four-wheel-drive version, they wrote: "We like cars that you can't put immediately into a narrow mental category. We like to let our imagination run free sometimes, so that the articles we use match them-

The third Civic model generation, sold between 1983 and 1987, was notable for its clear, well-defined outlines: these are the two-door sedan and the Shuttle

The Honda CR-X was a 100-horsepower car that enlivened the market for small, low-priced sport coupes

selves to us and not the other way around. That's why we approve of the Honda Shuttle, particularly the 4WD version. Its styling isn't breathtakingly well-balanced, but we like the mental stimulus it provides. Is it the world's largest small car? Or the world's smallest multi-purpose vehicle? Is it just a station wagon with four-wheel drive? Whatever it is, the Civic Shuttle seems to satisfy all our wishes."

In 1983 it was the turn of auto, motor und sport to describe the CRX: "There's another offshoot of the Honda Civic that's distinctly faster and not as high off the ground. It also represents a new landmark in Honda's model policy. The Civic CRX Coupe aims to give the market for small, moderately priced sport coupes a new impetus." The autorevue, which is published in Vienna, Austria, described the Civic CRX as "an intelligent car that doesn't flaunt its virtues like teacher's pet but is there to satisfy our legitimate desire for a car that's fun to drive. Sixty horsepower make it a friendly boaster, eighty make it a bit of a confidence trickster, but a hundred earn it the recognition it deserves as a competent sports car."

INTERNATIONAL SUCCESS

Although the CRX and the Shuttle have done a lot for the Civic's image, it is none the less the hatchback and the sedan that have sold in quantity. More than eleven and a half million Civics have now been produced, making it the company's most popular model. The third-generation Civic, launched in 1983 and produced until a successor appeared in the fall of 1987, contributed a lot to this success story.

In a comparative road test including the hatchback version of the 1.5i GT, the magazine auto, motor und sport wrote: "The Civic creates a feeling of interior space by virtue of the extra distance between the windshield and the front seats. The body extremities are easy for the driver to see and the seated position behind the small-diameter steering wheel is as low-slung and sporty as in a genuine sports car." Later, the magazine again comments on the "surprising sense of space", and explains: "It results not only from generous body width but also from moving the windshield forward as far as possible. Those who occupy the front seats have ample space for their shoulders and elbows, and plenty of headroom too."

In April 1986 the CRX Coupé was given a new engine and launched on the German market as the Civic CRX 1.6i-16. The price now included a 1.6-liter engine with four valves per cylinder and an output of 125 hp. The top speed went up from about 190 km/h (118 mph) to almost 210 km/h (130 mph), and the 100 km/h (62 mph) acceleration mark was reached in 8.4 seconds.

In the meantime, Honda not only had a further Civic model generation under development, that was presented to the public in the fall of the following year at the German Motor Show in Frankfurt, but also introduced a new Accord in 1985 – and its long-awaited top model, the Legend.

Since 1976 about 2,700,000 Accords had been manufactured, and with the latest model generation Honda was determined to become, in the words of Takeo Okusa, then General Manager of Honda Deutschland, "the Japanese automaker with a place in Germany's upper midsize car segment". In clearer terms, the aim was to challenge Audi, BMW and Mercedes-Benz on their own ground.

The first move was to launch two variations on the Accord theme: a notchback sedan with three alternative engines (65 kW/88 hp 1.6-liter, 78 kW (106 hp) 2-liter and also a 2-liter fuel-injection engine rated at 90 kW (122 hp). Another new departure was a sedan in station-wagon style named the Aerodeck, which was only offered with one of the two-liter engines. The engines once again featured Honda's successful 12-valve cylinder heads. In an interim assessment after 30,000 kilometers (19,000 miles) of its long-term test, the magazine mot described these

The German car magazine auto, motor und sport described the Aerodeck as: "an unusually styled proposal for a car between a station wagon and a coupe"

engines as "agile and free-revving". Other points scored by the Accord in this test were for its easy gear shift action, generous interior space, good build quality, comfortable seats, powerful lights and the large number of sensible details in its equipment specification.

The tester's conclusions: "We were almost glad when the fuel filler flap wouldn't close any more and a clumsy driver broke off the rather flimsy key for the radio security lock. Otherwise we would have nothing negative at all to say about this exceptionally reliable car, that's ideal for everyday driving. What have the doubters to say now, with their garish pictures of the second-class Japanese car? So far, every single journey we have made in this car has proved them wrong."

The autorevue magazine came to a similar conclusion, though expressed in slightly less formal terms: "Whatever the question you ask, the Honda Accord is the perfect schoolchild who has done his homework well. How is one to assess such a car that wriggles out of any form of criticism – it's like trying to catch a trout with one's bare hands! The Accord is not exposed to attack anywhere, and attempts to pin even few shortcomings onto it are doomed to failure: there's no way of piercing its armored shell of perfection."

On the Aerodeck coupe version, the auto, motor und sport magazine had this to say: "Following the example of the Civic, Honda has now introduced an Accord Aerodeck. In the hierarchy of Honda's current midsize models, this unusually styled car occupies a

position somewhere between conventional station wagon and coupe. The 'Aerodeck' name is evidently intended to emphasize the generous glass areas, particularly at the rear, that make this version of the Accord light and airy inside as well as elegant." The magazine commented on the engine in the following terms: "The two-liter engine is surely one of the finest that Nippon's young engineers have so far produced. It responds perfectly to gas pedal movement and revs freely without any feeling that pulling power is lacking at lower engine speeds."

In 1987 another new Civic model generation appeared, and once again four different versions were offered to the public: four-door sedan, two-door station wagon, Shuttle 4WD and sporty CRX Coupe. At their very first presentation, it was obvious that the new Civic models were attractively styled additions to the Honda model program. With their smooth, elegant outlines the two- and four-door sedans and the CRX were a hit with the public at the Frankfurt Motor Show; the latest Shuttle 4WD had to wait for the next year's Geneva Show for its debut.

The Süddeutsche Zeitung newspaper made a detour into Honda's company history before commenting on the new Civic: "Whoever heard of a company with people reaching key management positions before the age of forty, and becoming senior executives before they are fifty? Especially in Japan, where appoint-

Starting in 1987, the fourth-generation Civic models kept the Honda dealers' showrooms busy.

The two- and four-door sedans and the Shuttle were once again attractively styled

With its Legend Coupe of 1987 the Japanese company took the bold step of entering the large luxury car class. With its restrained styling this model was a great success in the USA, whereas the Europeans took some time to become accustomed to Japanese competition in this car class

ments to company directorships normally go only to sixty-year-olds! Honda is the exception – and rumor has it that the old guard regard this progressive company as a subsersive 'red cell'. Honda sends its young engineers and designers forth all over the world to see what the others are doing – to California, Detroit and Europe. Not surprisingly, the company's products often seem more European than Japanese. The new Civic models are the best possible evidence of this. The four-door body is perhaps still a little unambitious or even dull, but the hatchback (with its station-wagon style of tailgate) has now become an exceptionally elegant car that could easily have emerged from an Italian design studio. Three engines are on offer to drive these new models: a 55-kW (75-hp)

1.3-liter, a 66-kW (90-hp) version of 1.4 liters' capacity and, for the top version, a 1.6-liter fuel injection engine developing 80 kW (109 hp)."

The newspaper continued: "Does the Civic stand a chance on our market? The answer is probably yes. It looks good (particularly the two-door hatch) and its performance is equally good for the price charged. The Civic is clear evidence that Honda builds the most European of all Japanese cars – we must expect plenty more interesting developments from this particular manufacturer!"

Almost two months after the Civic's presentation, journalists were able to get their hands on the latest CRX. The CRX 1.6i-16 version

132

went on sale shortly after this at 25,490 German Marks. The magazine auto, motor und sport had further details for its readers: "The CRX is the only model in the new Civic line with a double overhead camshaft engine. The others have four valves as well, but operated by a single overhead camshaft. The 1,600 cc unit in the CRX now develops 130 horsepower and is one of the keys to the car's top speed of 212 km/h (132 mph). Another is certainly the good aerodynamics of the CRX's low-slung, more curvaceous body."

Since its first appearance in September 1983 the CRX had gained Honda a respectable position in this market segment. In the company's own press release we read: "As a sporty, lively 'driving machine' the CRX

stands out prominently in the Honda model program. Its popularity with the public is not only due to its individual, advanced styling but also to the value for money it offers, which is almost unequaled for a thoroughbred sports car such as this."

The ams authors were more impressed by the improvement in comfort: "The CRX is not only more streamlined now but more comfortable too. The wheelbase is longer, which benefits the interior space situation. Driver and front passenger certainly travel first class, whereas it's difficult to imagine the rear seat of this 2+2 model being used for anything except emergency luggage-carrying." The autorevue, on the other hand, put the emphasis on driving pleasure: "Large sports cars may be faster, more luxurious and more imposing than this. But small sports cars are more fun. The Civic family consists of Papa Shuttle, Mama Sedan, a chic daughter in the form of a two-door hatchback – and this mad little brother, the CRX. The sports-car angle is emphasized indirectly by leaving off everything that a sports car out not to have. Electric windows? Central locking? Who needs them, provided that the interior is trimmed in black and the steering wheel is pleasant to hold. (It is – in fact it's even adjustable for height!) The Civic CRX is strictly speaking a two seater that fits the body like a glove."

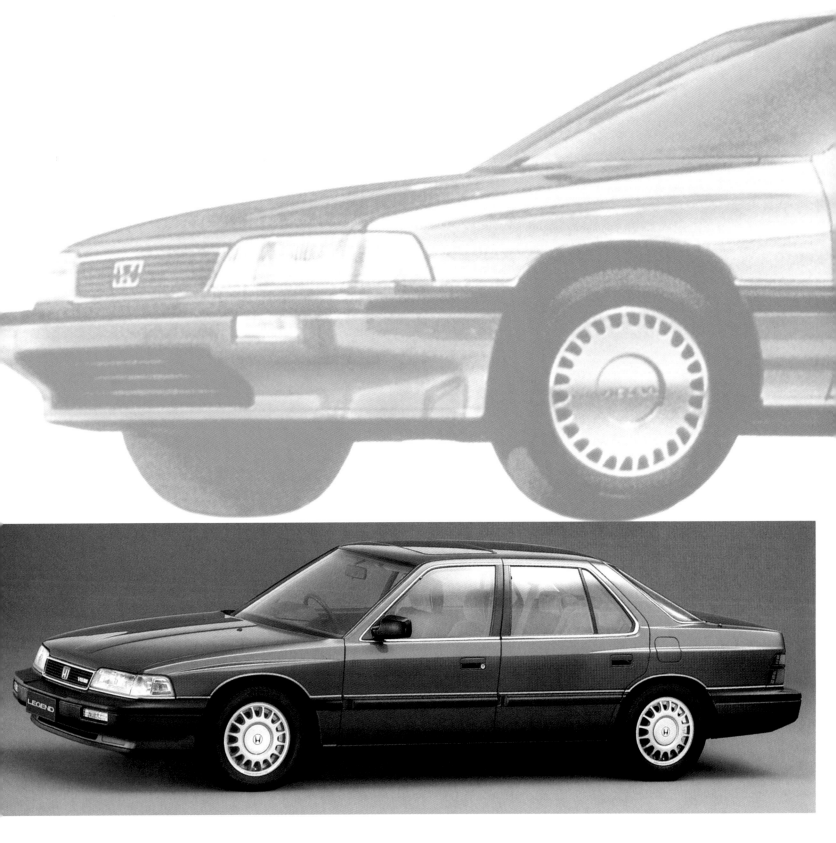

After the new CRX had appeared, the new Civic model program was effectively complete, except for the latest edition of the Shuttle which was not shown to the public until the Brussels Motor Show in mid-January 1988. Honda labeled its Shuttle 4WD a 'versatile leisure sedan'. With four doors, it was propelled by an 80-kW (109-hp) 1,6-liter 16-valve engine and had permanent four-wheel drive. Now that Honda had clearly established itself firmly in the midsize segment of the car market, it was clearly only a question of time before it made an onslaught on the next important bastion of the automobile establishment: the large luxury sedan. To take up a position on a level with European representatives of this class, with their many years of tradition and their high-tech image,

134

was clearly difficult without a corresponding change in Honda's public image. After all, high-tech and everything it signified was also in demand in Japan.

We have already seen how Soichiro Honda in his unconventional way often allowed his young management team free rein to an extent that would have been unthinkable in other companies. Added to this, Honda himself, the founder of the company, was a technical man who always gave precedence to what his engineers had to say.

It came as no surprise when Honda identified the need for high-tech and high quality as the correct combination for the future. It was also clear how the company intended to tell an international public without delay where it should look for leading-edge technology. The answer: motor sport – and in particular Formula One, the top motor racing category that regularly drew many millions of people to their TV sets all over the world. The whole

Honda team put every possible effort into this new project, with a view to showing the automobile world that Europeans and Americans were not the only ones capable of producing a high-tech racing engine. The experiment paid off, as narrated elsewhere in this book.

In the final analysis, however, motor sport is only an effective promotional measure if one also has the 'hardware', the standard model range, to go with it. As so often, Honda went its own way in this respect. The first evidence came at an early stage in the form of its co-operation with British Leyland. The reasons were obvious: Leyland and Honda were two companies that fitted together well and had identical interests. The British were looking for a partner with adequate financial resources and engine know-how; Honda in turn now had an opportunity to establish its first European production base, following the exceptionally successful plants already in operation in the USA.

The 150-horsepower Legend sedan received favorable criticism from the very start – but coupled with the desire for a more powerful engine. This too appeared before long

135

INTERNATIONAL SUCCESS

For this form of cooperation the auto, motor und sport magazine found an unexpectedly poetic description: "Even in the hard-fought mercantile territory between Japan and Europe there is evidently room for an 'economic biotope' – as proved by the contracts exchanged between the Honda Motor Corporation and the Austin Rover Group." And commenting on the new project for a luxury model: "The Japanese-British duet hopes to continue the results achieved so far with the Triumph Acclaim and the Rover 200 models by producing an upper midsize car. Honda's R&D Center in Tochigi has created a six-cylinder model that will be sold in Japan as the Honda Legend and will reach Europe in the fall of 1986 badged as a Rover."

In connection with the Legend, the German newspaper Süddeutsche Zeitung came up with the headline: "Now to Show the Europeans!", and continued: "There was a time when the Japanese had to fear being forced off the European car market by the imposition of sales quotas. This situation gave rise to such joint ventures as that between Honda and Rover. To this we owe the Rover 800 and the Honda Legend, which differ mainly in their bodies. The engine (2,493 cc, 110 kW/ 150 hp, good for 0-100 km/h (0-62 mph) acceleration in 8.9 seconds and a top speed of 203 km/h/ 126 mph), the transmission and the running gear are always supplied by Honda. Whereas the Rover deliberately clings to that company's tradition, with plenty of leather and wood trim and an equal amount of understatement, the Legend looks more of a piece, and the Coupe to be available in the fall is an even more pleasant sight."

Honda was naturally well aware that sales of a Japanese car in the upper price category (43,800 Marks in Germany) would not take off immediately. It therefore decided that only selected dealers should stock the car initially, with an overall sales target of 1,500 units in the first year. In other words, the market was to be opened up steadily and without hurrying things. The newspaper commented as follows: "It's difficult to forecast what sort of a future the Honda Legend will enjoy – it has no fundamental flaws, the styling may not appeal to everyone and the engine runs roughly at high speeds. There may also be some anxiety about buying a car that has been put together in an English factory with the casual approach for which British workers have become notorious. This can be dispelled, however, by stating that Japanese foremen drive every car round a special test track before it is allowed to leave the factory. For its price the Legend offers a gratifyingly complete equipment specification, with the automatic transmission and air conditioning as the only significant accessories needing to be ordered separately.

The Legend Coupe followed after a relatively brief interval – and the media were unanimous in declaring that it was a pointer to the

direction that the Japanese would take in their flight away from sheer volume production. Whereas Honda's sedan-model flagship was regarded as a car of relatively conventional concept, the 2+2-seater Legend Coupe was praised as a amazingly complete, successful design. Some writers, for instance ams, regretted the absence of a V8 engine, "but otherwise this mixture of well-proven components usually hits the nail on the head exactly."

The only critism, as implied above, was that the 2.5-liter engine tended to lack pulling power. Honda's technical people took this to heart and lost no time in increasing the engine size to 2.7 liters, which boosted the power output from 150 to 169 hp (124 kW) and also upped the peak torque to 230 Nm. As a result of the power hike and better initial response, the 24-valve unit proved to be altogether more agreeable in this mutated form. Despite the Legend Coupe's high tare weight of 1.4 tons, it now accelerated from 0 to 100 km/h (62 mph) in only 7.9 seconds and reached a top speed of 210 km/h (130.5 mph). In ams one could now read: "The generously equipped Legend Coupe is turning itself into a competitor for Mercedes – a sign that Honda is the first Japanese manufacturer for whom nothing is sacrosanct, not even the distinguished large luxury car category in which German manufacturers have always held the lion's share."
Potential customers for the four-door sedan

naturally began to ask themselves why the 2.7-liter engine should be reserved for those who chose the Coupe – they clamored for the larger engine sufficiently loudly for their complaints to be heard in far-away Tokyo, and after a reasonable delay the marketing people there decided to relent and sell the sedan too with the 2.7-liter engine.

Another of Honda's high-tech sensations was its 4WS system - an abbreviation for 'four-wheel steering' Experiments of this nature had been conducted as long ago as before the Second World War, but mainly for military clients who wanted their vehicles to remain as maneuverable as possible on rough terrain. Honda was the first company to make such a system available on volume-produced cars (and also of course in a form suitable for high road speeds). In Germany, Honda was accordingly the first manufacturer of road-going automobiles to apply for and be granted a general operating permit for a four-wheel steering system from the Federal German Road Vehicles Office.

The latest edition of the well-established Prelude was chosen to introduce the four-wheel steering system, on which tthe rear wheels responded to the angle taken up by those at the front. Under the heading 'The Modern Coupe Concept', the press folder had the following to say: "Now that the Prelude has proved to be such a successful model, this Coupe concept has been subjected to system-

At the end of the 1980s Honda offered its Prelude with the world's first four-wheel steering system controlled by the angle of the front wheels

atic further development for the 1988 model year. Two engines have been chosen to propel it: the EX model uses an 80-kW (109-hp) two-liter unit with alloy block and three valves per cylinder, giving it a top speed of over 180 km/h (112 mph). The Prelude 16V is powered by a DOHC 16-valve engine rated at 101 kW (137 hp) and has a top speed of over 200 km/h (124 mph)."

But as we have said, the real sensation on the Prelude was its four-wheel steering: "The new Prelude is the first series-production car in the world to be available with Honda's 4WS system, which turns the rear wheels in response to the steering angle of the front wheels. A mechanically actuated rear-wheel steering box moves the rear wheels either in the same direction as at the front or in the opposite direction, depending on the amount of lock applied at the steering wheel by the driver. This system assures optimum handling and maneuvering characteristics and represents a substantial gain in safety."

The Süddeutsche Zeitung commented: "For customers with ample cash in their piggy banks there is a high-tech version that not only brakes all four wheels but steers them too. At last there is a car that can manage what any not totally unintelligent four-legged animal has always been able to do in its sleep, so to speak. Honda's patented four-wheel steering is a purely mechanical one that turns the rear wheels one way or the other according to the steering angle at the front. The obvious question is: do we need it? The equally obvious answer: yes and no!"

With the Legend and the Prelude – above all the 4WS version – Honda staked its claim to a place in the high-tech category. The next step was clearly the introduction of the latest version of the Civic, which was due for its world premiere in September 1988 at the German 'IAA' in Frankfurt. As expected, each of the four versions of the third-generation Civic convinced intending buyers with its clear lines and agreeable styling. The hatchback with its wide-opening tailgate was still the car for city dwellers; the sedan had developed more and more into a family car that deserved to be taken very seriously. The Shuttle, in turn, with its highly versatile interior, appealed to larger families and those who practiced sport in their leisure time. Last but not least, the CRX continued to fulfill the part of the small sports car to perfection. There were no basic changes to the 1.3- and 1.6-liter four-cylinder engines, which continued to develop 55 and 97 kW (75 and 130 hp).

A year later the Concerto reached the market, another model developed jointly with Leyland. Despite its musical name it failed to harmonize to any great extent with customers' wishes, and its career lasted fewer than four years. For Honda's potential buying public it seems to have been too conservative in its styling. The Concerto was powered by engines of 1.5 or 1.6 liters developing 91 and 120 horsepower.

In June 1990 Nobuhiko Kawamoto became Honda's chief executive officer, an engineer who had been one of the people responsible for the company's magnificent motor racing victories and, as head of the development department for many years, one of the driving forces behind Honda's success. With his decision to allow the various Honda companies around the world to operate more independently, without direct control from Japan, Kawamoto was largely responsible for ensuring that Honda established itself as the most international of all Japanese-based companies. Today only one third of Honda's total workforce are Japanese – the remainder come from the 34 countries in which the company has production facilities and also from the more than 160 countries in which these products are sold internationally.

A cosmopolitan personality, Kawamoto was also the guiding hand behind the NSX, of which a prototype was first shown in February 1989 zu sehen war. More than a year elapsed before this mid-engined, all-aluminium sports car started production in the summer of 1990, and potential customers were therefore obliged for a considerable time to study the sparse information released about this car with its 201-kW (274-hp) three-liter V6 engine, which many journalists saw as Japan's first worthy rival to Ferrari.

After comparing it with the Ferrari 348 in 1991, the Motor-Revue was moved to comment: "You must have driven the NSX before you can fairly say which car leads and the other follows. The Honda is a real surprise. It's safer to drive, more comfortable and less hard on the nerves than the Ferrari. It's also faster as the distance builds up. Those who yawn and make dismissive gestures are likely to miss the high spot of the day. Driving the NSX is fun, to a degree that makes one almost ashamed. It commands the entire repertoire of the classic sports car from the inspiringly free-revving engine to the direct road feel imparted by its suspension – and even the appropriate sports-car sound is there."

In November 1992 Honda announced the NSX-R for the Japanese market only, with the R standing for 'racing'. With its weight reduced by 130 kliograms (287 lbs) to 1,230 kilograms (2,712 lbs) and its 280-horsepower engine, it was capable of reaching the 280 km/h limit. Those who prefered an open car were satisfied from 1996 on by the NSX-T, with its removable roof panel. Currently the last stage in NSX evolution took place in January 1997, when the new 3.2-liter 24-valve V6 engine was presented at the Detroit Show; it has an output of 206 kW (280 hp).

Honda may have been strongly committed to demonstrating its engineering skills with this supersport coupe, but the other vehicles in its

model program were not being neglected. In the fall of 1989 the CRX acquired a new engine, which later appeared in other models as well. It was known as the VTEC, an abbreviation derived from its variable camshaft timing. A 1.6-liter four-cylinder unit, its two camshafts could be reset according to the power output needed; the peak figure was an impressive 110 kW (150 hp), capable of propelling the car up to an impressive 222 km/h (138 mph) top speed and at the same time of achieving very satisfactory fuel economy.

In the fall of 1990 it was time for a second version of the Legend and the associated Coupe model. The extremely elegant styling was retained, but the six-cylinder engine was enlarged to 3.2 liters and developed 151 kW (205 hp). A jump forward to March 1996 brings us to the third-generation Legend, offered for sale only as a four-door sedan after production of the Coupe had been terminated.

Little changed externally, the new Legend was given a 151-kW (205-hp) V6 24-valve

The Honda NSX was acknowledged immediately as one of the world's great supersport models, aided by a six-cylinder engine willing to rev freely to high speeds, and developing 274 hp in its initial form

engine enlarged to 3.5 liters and capable of propelling this luxury sedan up to a top speed of 215 km/h (134 mph).

The fifth generation of Civic models was unveiled in the fall of 1991 at the German 'IAA' Motor Show in Frankfurt. As expected, the two-door hatchback and the four-door sedan were as restrained and elegant as ever in their styling. The corresponding CRX, which was launched in the spring of 1992, proved to be a coupe of a rather special kind: as an optional extra it could be obtained with

141

The dashboard of the
Honda NSX, which
was also available
from 1996 on as the
NSX-T, with a detachable
roof panel

In 1991 Honda introduced the fifth generation of its Civic model (see previous double page)

The second-generation Legend Coupé, launched in 1996, was even more restrained and elegant in its styling

With a 205-hp, 3.5-liter six-cylinder engine, the new Legend sedan had a top speed of 215 km/h (133 mph) and every possible luxury feature

a targa-style roof that retracted automatically into the area behind the seats at the driver's command. Further models joined the Civic program in later years: in 1993, for example, there was a Civic Coupe that made an interesting contrast with its classically elegant shape to the wiry, sporting CRX. In 1994 a four-door fastback version with large tailgate was added, and in 1995 the engines underwent a thorough design revision. They all had four valves per cylinder now, displacements extending from 1.4 to 1.6 liters and power outputs from 55 kW (75 hp) to

118 kW (160 hp), and as was only to be expected, they all combined plenty of performance with only a moderate thirst for fuel.

Even at the presentation, insiders were convinced that the Civic program was due for further development before long. The next in this series of highly interesting models was the fastback sedan of March 1997. A year later the elegant Aerodeck station wagon also appeared to complete the model program for the moment.

Honda was probably reluctant to allow the German Motor Show in Frankfurt to pass by in September 1991 without a new model: this was the Prelude in its latest much-revised form, with engines from 2.0 to 2.3 liters and power outputs from 98 kW (133 hp) to 136 kW (185 hp). Restyled in a very smooth but rather undramatic way, the new Prelude was positioned above the somewhat smaller Civic Coupe, and also retained Honda's electronically controlled four-wheel steering which still had no rivals on the market.

By October 1996, however, when the fifth-generation Prelude was introduced, the four-wheel steering had vanished from the standard specification (anyone who wanted it as an option was invited to pay the healthy sum of three thousand marks extra). This does not seem to have interfered with the success of the sharply styled Prelude at all: the first road tests were full of praise for this inter-esting coupe, which was available initially with a 2.0-liter, 16-valve engine developing 98 kW (133 hp) or a 2.2-l 16-valve unit rated at 136 kW (185 hp). The magazine ams praised the 2.2-liter version for its "good workmanship, free-revving four-valve engine, sporty performance and excellent handling." The list price in Germany was 49,580 Marks.

The new version of the Today model, first seen in January 1993 in Japan, had a three-cylinder, twelve-valve engine of only 657 cc and was clearly aimed at Japanese customers with their chronic parking-space problems. It was a cuddly four-seater with 35 kW (48 hp) of power at its disposal. On an international level the revised Accord model, presented in September 1993, was a more significant event. The fourth generation of this successful midsize sedan was available with the 101-kW (136-hp) or 140-kW (190-hp) four-

Over the years the Civic – this is a fifth-generation car – developed into a timeless classic with satisfied owners all over the world

147

148

In 1996 Honda revised the Prelude Coupé's design again (front); just for a change, the Civic models in the background have only a supporting role to play in this picture

Plenty of load space: the Honda Civic Aerodeck, seen here as the 1998 model

Another Honda model that has acquired classic status over the years: the Accord, first offered in September 1993 with engines developing between 136 and 190 hp

cylinder engines from the Prelude, making it faster, with a top speed of up to 215 km/h (134 mph) than its understated appearance suggested. For the USA, an Accord Coupe appeared very soon, and also a station wagon bearing the familiar 'Aerodeck' name and also available as an option with the Legend's 2.7-liter six-cylinder engine rated at 127 kW (172 hp). This version never made it across the Atlantic to European markets.

In 1996 this model line received a facelift, with smoother body panels and new front-end styling. The engines were also modified and given four valves per cylinder in all cases. To make it quite clear that the Accord was still the Civic's bigger brother, they had displacements of 1,850 cc (85 kW/ 116 hp), 1,997 cc (97 kW/ 131 hp) and 2,156 cc (110 kW/

*Subsequent Accord
model generations
were even longer
and more elegant in
their styling – this is
a 1996 model*

*For people who need a
lot of load-carrying
space and also like to
sit higher – the Honda
Civic Shuttle*

152

150 hp). The ams magazine summed up: "Inside the new Accord, it's several degrees more comfortable than in its predecessor – the suspension filters out minor road roughness effectively and noise from the engine and road are kept to a low level."

In the spring of 1994 Honda's corporate policy was obliged to take an unexpected turn, when the British partner Rover was bought by BMW. The Bavarians spent about a billion German Marks on acquiring Rover, and left Honda with no other choice but to withdraw from the jointly developed projects that were currently in hand. As a sign that this did not mean abandoning activities in Europe. Honda's plant in Swindon, England, was therefore enlarged continuously in the next few years. Its potential output has gone up from 108,000 vehicles in 1997 to a scheduled 250,000 in the year 2002. Honda invested about about 700 million dollars in this extension project in 1998, and Swindon is now working in close cooperation with the Research and Development Center in Offenbach, Germany, on the latest successor to the Honda Civic and on a small car specially planned for European driving conditions.

Honda's technical experts naturally surveyed the market carefully in recent years in order to identify additional types of vehicle that could enrich the model program. They found that customers were still interested in a successor to the legendary Shuttle, which had a firm following in Europe although it never sold in large numbers. In response to this evident demand, a new Shuttle generation appeared in October 1994, with a 107 kW (145-hp) 2.3-liter 16-valve engine and a top speed of 185 km/h (115 mph). A minivan that was none the less 4.75 meters (187 inches) long, its interior space was naturally very generous, extremely variable in layout and,

thanks to four doors and a large tailgate, easy to load and unload.

Another market niche was filled in October 1995 by the CR-V, presented at the Paris Show. An off-road vehicle with permanent all-wheel drive, it could tackle anything from sandy coastlines to snow-covered mountains. The power came from a 97-kW (130-hp) two-liter four-cylinder engine, but of course the large frontal area and unavoidably high drag coefficient limited top speed to 160 km/h (100 mph). The first road impressions concluded that the 'Comfortable Runabout Vehicle' (we must presumably believe it when we are told that this is what the initials stand for) earned its name in every respect.

A model of less interest for the European market is the Logo, launched in October 1996; with a 1,343-cc engine developing 49 kW (67 hp), it is mainly sold in Asia.

The CR-V was Honda's first venture into the off-road market: a 130-hp, 2-liter four-cylinder engine propelled this all-wheel-drive vehicle

With permanent four-wheel drive, the CR-V was Honda's first off-road model (previous double page)

A 1.4-liter, 67-horse-power engine made the Honda Logo an agile car

The Integra, various versions of which have been sold in Japan and the USA since 1985, came to Europe much later. The Integra Type R 1.8 16V reached the dealers' showrooms in 1997 as a particularly sporting version of this model. It not only had a 140-kW (190-hp) engine but also an impressive rear wing as a sign to all concerned that it was a sports model that demanded to be taken seriously.

Another exciting development in these months was when the interested public came to realize that Honda fully intended to market its SSM – the initials standing for Sports Study Model – as the new Honda S 2000. The show car had received its world premiere at the Tokyo Motor Show in October 1995 and was a highly emotive roadster. The Honda company, searching for a suitable present to celebrate its own 50th birthday in the fall of 1998, settled on this model – a most welcome choice.

With its clearly defined outlines, restrained wedge-shaped body and high-performance engine, the S 2000 soon became a favorite among car journalists, who regarded it as the legitimate successor to the legendary Honda S 800. But whereas the latter car's tiny 791-cc engine developed 67 hp at 7,570 rpm. the 2-liter four-cylinder engine in the S 2000 is allowed to rev not only to a remarkable 8,300

rpm, at which speed it produces 176 kW (240 rpm), but in fact to an even more awe-inspiring 9,000 rpm before the limit is reached. A completely new development, this compact double overhead-camshaft unit delivers its maximum torque of 208 Nm at an engine speed of 7,500 rpm.

Such power naturally has no trouble in propelling the S 2000, which weighs 1,260 kilograms (2,645 lbs) in a spirited manner. The top speed is 241 km/h (149.7 mph) and the 100 km/h (62 mph) mark is passed from a standstill after only 6.2 seconds. Nor is this roadster a stripped-down model more suited to the racetrack; on the contrary, it is a fully-equipped two-seater that can be driven all the year round, and has a electrically operated soft top (an aluminum hardtop is also available for the winter season). The leather used for the sport seat upholstery is even specially treated to resist exposure to bright sunlight and rain. The standard transmission is a six-speed gearbox with a precise, light action manual shift. The red starter button with its chrome surround is a nostalgic reminiscence of a classic motor sport tradition.

The S 2000's power to weight ratio of only 5.25 horsepower per kilogram, and its suspension, borrowed and suitably tamed from competition car design principles, are among the keys to the exceptional pleasure this car provides, though its true limits are surely only to be found on the racing circuit.

With its S 2000, of which it is planned to build only 16,000 units annually, Honda has once again permitted itself the pleasure of building a car that dealers and customers will be desperate to get their hands on; for instance, Honda in Germany is unlikely to be allocated more than 600 cars a year. But each of these compact roadsters will be ample evidence that Honda has, as always, a soft spot in its heart for everyone who derives true pleasure from opening the garage door and seeing exceptional technologies packed in such an attractive way.

In September 1998 Honda held a presentation in Japan for a further new model, the HR-V. The unusual styling of this 'leisure-mobile' has attracted considerable attention. The high body, wihch is none the less well laid out from the driver's point of view, conceals a 1.6-liter, 77-kW (105-hp) four-cylinder engine which is coupled either to a five-speed manual gearbox or a CVT (continuously vari-

Sassy and stylish: the small Honda Logo was mainly designed for the Asian market, but also went on sale in various European countries

The 190-hp Integra-R was powerful enough for motor racing with few modifications

In view of Japan's land shortage, manufacturers will continue to develop ultra-compact vehicles like the Life microvan of 1997 or the Z Coupe dating from 1970 (next double page)

able transmission). The HR-V's top speeds with these two drivelines are quoted as 165 km/h (102.5 mph) and 157 kph (97.5 mph) respectively. In all normal driving conditions, the HR-V is content to drive the front wheels only, but the driveline also extends rearwards and cuts in automatically if grip deteriorates, thus contributing to safe progress. The body's attractive looks, the generous interior space and the moderate price asked for the HR-V have gained it a large number of loyal customers almost immediately.

With cars such as the HR-V or the S 2000, Honda has opened the door to emotion in car design once again, after a number of years in which common-sense predominated – though an exception should be made for the already legendary NS-X. This change of heart is most welcome, because a major automobile company should not only sell its products but

also dreams as a means of making our everyday lives more agreeable.

Honda today is, if all its divisions are added together, the world's largest manufacturer of motorcycles, motor scooters, automobiles, agricultural machinery, power generating sets and boats. In the past 50 years it has produced no fewer than one hundred million motorcycles.

In 1997 Honda for the first time manufactured more than two million vehicles and ten million engines.

It is a company that grew within half a century into one of the few genuinely global corporations in existence today – because its farsighted founder soon realized that international success was impossible to achieve if the products took no heed of national re-

Unusually styled, the HR-V lies midway between station wagon and coupe; it has front-wheel drive, but drive to the rear wheels is engagcd automatically on poor roads or if driving conditions are bad. The upper picture shows the four-door version, which starts production in the summer of 2000

159

quirements. 'Think global – act local' was the slogan that has made Soichiro Honda's company just slightly different from any other Japanese manufacturer – a company that has attracted people from many other countries too and which, led by Hiroyuki Yoshino since he took over the chief executive's post from Nobuhiko Kawamoto in the summer of 1998, must be regarded as one of the most successful manufacturers of automobiles and motorcycles of all time and anywhere in the world.

With its S 2000, Honda has created a sporty, elegant roadster powered by a 240 hp double overhead camshaft two-liter, four-cylinder engine that can reach speeds of up to 9,000 rpm

Honda's designers and technicians are not unusual in wanting to display their interesting new ideas from time to time. The J-VX design study of 1997 has a one-liter three-cylinder engine, and also features the IAM system. This is a disc-shaped electric motor between the engine and the clutch that charges the battery by absorbing energy when the car is braked, and supplies it again when additional acceleration is needed. A fuel consumption of only 3 liters per 100 km (78 US mpg) is claimed for the J-VX, which has an aluminum body

1,500 MINDS FOR FORMULA ONE

A S MR. HONDA SHOOK NIKI LAU-
DA'S HAND BEFORE THE 1982
LONG BEACH GRAND PRIX, THE AUS-
TRIAN ASKED QUITE SHAMELESSLY:
"WHEN ARE YOU GUYS COMING BACK
TO FORMULA ONE?"
MR. HONDA SMILED CRYPTICALLY AND
SAID IN ENGLISH: "I DON'T KNOW!"

The yardstick for the others: Ayrton Senna at the wheel of the Marlboro McLaren Honda in the 1990 season

At that time, Honda's 1.5-liter turbocharged engine had long since been running on the Japanese company's test benches.

Honda had put up with the domination of the German engines from Porsche and BMW for a relatively long time. In 1984, the first victory for the Honda-Wiliams "marriage" in Dallas was more or less coincidence. Keke Rosberg won the race by displaying the improvisatory talent of a rally driver on an asphalt surface that was breaking up and turning back into gravel. Things did not begin to change in any real sense until the 1984 Dutch Grand Prix in Zandvoort. There, Honda's chief of development, Nobuhiko Kawamoto, witnessed how Rosberg coasted to a stop with nothing but a damp patch in the bottom of the fuel tank, as Prost and Lauda shot past to another double victory in the McLaren TAG-Porsche Turbo. In this moment of utter humiliation, Kawamoto, lord over 7,000 engineers, decided that something would have to be done.

The Williams people have since revealed that Honda's spies got hold of the German Mahle company's pistons. This is an indication that the Japanese were not able to solve the piston problems encountered by their first turbo engines until they had access to German know-how – so much for methods reminiscent of the old New Year's Eve tradition of telling fortunes by pouring molten lead.

In mid-1985, Honda set up its own Engine Center next to the Williams factory in Did-

cot. Two dozen specialists toiled away there, assembling and servicing the racing turbos. This ant-like batallion – far away from home and (by our standards) poorly paid – helped Japan to win the Formula One turbo-war. Once a month, the Japanese visitors climbed into five cars and – lined up neatly one behind the other so that no one would get lost – drove from Didcot to a Japanese restaurant in London, where they assuaged their homesickness. In Didcot, they were accommodated in five rented houses.

Honda's Formula One offensive had built up a full head of steam in 1985. That summer, no less than 59 (repeat, 59!) engines were sacrificed in test drives alone. In the end, however, this paid off as far as reliability was concerned: the Honda engines were in a class by themselves.

Frank William's oracle seemed to be coming true. He had declared that the day would come when nobody would be able to compete with Honda. Not BMW, not Porsche, not Ferrari, not Renault. If Honda so wished, he added, it could put 1,500 minds to work on pulling the Formula One plow.

The 1986 Honda engine was quite conservative, Nigel Mansell recalls. "It was not made of aluminum (as was the Renault engine), which made it 25 kilograms heavier, and the ceramic conrods and oval pistons were not as good as they promised to be. Yet it must have had the lead as far as electronics were concerned – how could it otherwise have been

possible that Piquet and I always had fuel left over when Alain Prost had run out?"
Honda's telemetry produced more precise calculations than the competition could manage. The Japanese were also able to radio instructions to the driver telling him to enrich the mixture or make it leaner.
Since Honda was paying Nelson Piquet's salary – a healthy 3.3 million dollars even then – they expected him to take the title.

Needless to say, Nigel Mansell was not particularly pleased with this plan, and won five Grands Prix during the season.
As we know, it was Alain Prost in the Mc Laren-TAG Turbo who became World Champion with a two-point lead. This was due largely to the fact that Williams did not establish a team order, and Mansell's last chance for the title was lost because of a tire blowout in the Australian Grand Prix.

A brilliant team but not one without problems: Ayrton Senna und Alain Prost are seen here with Soichiro Honda

---

World champion in 1987: Nelson Piquet driving the Williams Honda

1500 MINDS FOR FORMULA ONE

Titles and trophies unlimited – the McLaren company's foyer with an impressive collection of Grand Prix cars

In September 1987, the news that had caused a stir weeks before became official: after 20 victories together, Honda dropped Williams in favor of McLaren.

Today, Frank Williams describes the situation after his accident by explaining that the Japanese were suddenly faced with a man who could not walk, who was "no longer the same person with whom they had signed the contract. Honda wrote me and my team off." In 1987, in the Williams, Honda power took Piquet to the world championship title ahead of Nigel Mansell. The fact that Mansell was still driving for Williams in 1987 was due to Honda's initiative: Williams would have preferred to get rid of the unpredictable Brit. In the summer of 1986, Mansell had signed a preliminary contract with Ferrari. Nevertheless, Honda demanded that Williams get Nigel back. Which he did: Mansell broke his Ferrari contract and Honda declared itself willing to not only pay Piquet's salary, but also Mansell's.

Tragedy struck Williams in this fateful year of 1986: Frank had the accident that was to put him in a wheelchair for the rest of his life. Ron Dennis, who had already negotiated with Honda in 1986, took advantage of the situation. In the summer of 1987, he succeeded in landing Ayrton Senna for the 1988 season. Senna was still driving for Lotus, and his unbelievable talent was a very good reason for Honda also to deliver engines to Lotus in 1987. But in the Lotus-Honda, Senna was regularly beaten by the Williams-Honda drivers.

Whereas McLaren still had to pay Porsche for every stage in engine development, Ron Dennis's team received the Honda engines free.

The Japanese deployed more minds, more money, more test benches, and more tests in order to develop Formula One's best turbocharged engine. They put more and more wood on the fire, and employed fascinating computer games, innovative materials and new quality-control methods. Whenever Ferrari believed it had finally caught up, Honda broke away again with more innovations.

In 1988, the last turbo year, the McLaren-Honda victory machine was not to be stopped. In that season – with boost pressure reduced to 2.5 bar and fuel tank capacity to 150 liters – Senna and Prost drove with what we might call a "miraculous multiplication" of fuel. McLaren-Honda won 15 of the 16 races. Senna took pole position 13 times and won eight races. Prost took the pole twice and won seven times. Prost won all the races in which Senna had problems. There was a lot of talk back then about whether Honda had manipulated Senna's electronics in Estoril and Jerez (where Prost won) so that the world championship title would not be decided until the Japanese Grand Prix in Suzuka.

During a short vacation trip to Bali, Senna, who had just become World Champion, told me back then: "There was no manipulation. I never accepted that version. This is my second season working with Honda, and I've learned to understand the Japanese. I know their mentality. They would never have put the image they had earned in Formula One at risk by attempting any kind of manipulation. What really happened to me was a combination of various factors. I was still driving the car that had been involved in the collision with Schlesser in Monza. The crash had led to some shifts in the nose that were not visible, but caused handling problems and increased fuel consumption."

In the 1989 season, the Senna-Prost team (which McLaren chief Ron Dennis had looked after so well) broke up. Senna took Prost apart; 1989 was the first year of the new naturally aspirated formula.

Though driving the same car, Prost was no longer able to keep up with Senna, and therefore began a psychological war: he appealed to the public with his complaints and went so far as to accuse Honda of mobilizing more power for Senna than for himself. Honda, which otherwise operated in total secrecy, produced the critical computer printouts, which showed that Prost lost time against Senna on fast, break-neck sections of the cir-

It takes such magnificent ghosted drawings as these to reveal to the non-expert just what goes on inside a Formula One car; this is the title-winner of the 1987 season

cuit (such as the second Lesmo bend in Monza, where he was 24 km/h slower than Senna).

Ron Dennis backed Honda: If Prost did not set up his car as well as Senna, that was "his problem." The fact that the top speeds were identical showed that Honda was "playing fair." Prost countered by declaring that Honda could manipulate everything, including computer printouts. Senna remained silent and expressed himself in the language that he mastered best: performance.

As a result of the Prost-Senna collision in Suzuka, the Frenchman became World Champion in 1989. Prost switched from McLaren to Ferrari, and as a big Senna fan, Gerhard Berger signed up with McLaren for 1990.

After visiting Honda's Research & Development Center, Berger concluded: "When Ferrari has a problem, it can turn to the Fiat Development Department in Turin for help. But Ferrari is too proud to make such requests. Honda's racing engines, however, all come from this Development Center. The room is so big, you can't see where it ends. There are hundreds of engineers sitting there. One hands over his computer printout to the other. They do not have any distance to overcome like the one between Maranello and Turin. And if a problem arises on a Monday, a thousand engineers spend the whole week solving it."

"Honda" assured ex-Porsche engineer Ralf Hahn, who was then with Ferrari, "has a time edge that is hard to catch up with, particularly if you are still thinking about solutions that the Japanese already have. You can only close this gap with solutions that Honda does not have."

Honda's Chief of Development Kawamoto was at pains to put this effort into perspective. When asked how many engineers it took to design the V-10 cylinder engine, he replied: "Ten or fifteen, I would say. You don't need many more and it's not good to have too many. Most of the work is done by just three people – without a computer, just with slide rules or calculators. They go without sleep when they work on a project like that. If you have fifteen people, they sleep too much! But social structures in Japan are a lot different now from what they were ten or fifteen years ago. Our people are now union members, and they work eight hours a day."

At McLaren, Berger saw something he had never experienced before: "Honda came up with more power every two weeks!"

For Honda, Formula One was a training camp for young engineers sharpening their minds in the midst of gunsmoke and time pressure. In group work, learning processes were gone through in quick time. Early each morning, fifteen to twenty technicians appeared, powered up their wall-to-wall computers, the monitors began to glow and the men from Japan were logged into their computer files

like bookmarks – yet this was in an era when the digital age was still on the back burner for the other teams.

Senna and Berger were given computer diagrams that were enhanced to become tachograph print-outs of their individual laps. When superimposed, everyone could see who was faster or slower, and precisely where. Not even at Ferrari did Berger have such good comparisons, even if the tangled mass of data from telemetry or on-board computers was greater than with Honda.

All this success was founded on the sheer discipline and zealousness of the Honda engineers' work and their precision and collective knowledge. Despite all the electronic databases, the Japanese engineers involved the McLaren drivers in their task to an amazingly high degree. Gerhard Berger discloses a secret: "Honda wanted to know things from me about my engine that nobody even asked me about at Ferrari."

In 1990 and 1991, the brilliant Ayrton Senna became World Champion in the McLaren-Honda. In 1992, McLaren had a poorer overall package. For years, McLaren drew its superiority from a superior Honda engine. Nevertheless, in the meantime, Renault had also caught up. For years, McLaren had managed the Honda power perfectly, and multiplied it with Senna. But busy with all the victories, they missed boat on the next innovations. The McLaren aerodynamics built up

too much resistance and too little traction. Nor did they wake up in time to develop active wheel suspension.

As early as December 1991, Honda President Kawamoto had indicated to Ron Dennis that they would leave Formula One at the end of 1992. In December of 1991, Kawamoto was able to foresee what the end of the fiscal year (March 1992) would bring – a considerable drop in profits.

Since 1987, Honda had won everything there was to win. They had applied themselves to engine construction, and for 80 million dollars a year, they revealed a level of technical competence that hurt the other manufacturers deeply. Honda was only able to justify the expense with a clear carryover from Formula One to series production. The motorcycle giant had succeeded in building up the desired image in the automobile sector as well.

In 1992, McLaren fell so far behind Williams that not even Honda was able to close the gap with a new 12-cylinder engine.

Nigel Mansell became World Champion in a Williams-Renault.

On September 11, 1992, Honda announced in Monza that it would withdraw from Formula One at the end of the year.

There were new priorities to be set: environmental regulations, lean-combustion engines, and alternative drivelines. The engineers that were trained in Formula One were given new tasks.

At the peak of his career: Ayrton Senna with the 1991 McLaren-Honda. It was at the end of 1992 that Honda announced its withdrawal from Formula One

171

HONDA IN FORMULA 1

T HE HISTORY OF HONDA'S INVOLVEMENT IN MOTOR RACING BEGAN WELL BEFORE THE COMPANY WAS FOUNDED. IN 1924, AT THE AGE OF 18, SOICHIRO HONDA BUILT HIS OWN TWO-SEATER RACING CAR, THE CURTISS, NAMED FOR ITS V8 AERO ENGINE. ALTHOUGH THIS AMERICAN-BUILT ENGINE HAD A DISPLACEMENT OF 8.2 LITERS, ITS OUTPUT WAS ON THE MODEST SIDE: 90 HORSEPOWER AT 1400 RPM. NEVERTHELESS, HONDA'S CURTISS REACHED A CREDITABLE 100 MPH AND PERFORMED RELIABLY FOR SEVERAL YEARS.

HONDA IN FORMULA 1

World champion Jack Brabham took Honda on to the Formula 2 winners' podium in 1966. His Honda-engined cars won 11 races in succession

Honda then took a long break from motor sport. It was only in the early sixties, when Honda motorcycles were already chasing the world title, that the company, which was then planning to produce cars, decided to participate in four-wheeled forms of motor sport. Right from the start, Honda was determined to enter Formula 1 racing, but the first taste of success came in Formula 2 with Jack Brabham's team. Honda provided him with a one-liter four-cylinder four-valve engine – designed by Tadashi Kume – and sent the young Nobuhiko Kawamoto to England with it as racing engineer. After more than thirty years, Kawamoto still remembers the rather bitter lesson he learnt from the first race: "We retired on the starting line, because I'd fitted the wrong clutch!" After that, things went much better: Brabham won 11 races in succession with the small 150 bhp (110 kW) engine.

Honda's first few attempts at Formula 1 were nowhere near as successful, despite the then engine-size limit of 1500 cc, a distinct advan-

In 1964 Soichiro Honda tried everything in his power to break into Formula 1, but even five years of determined work failed to bring the anticipated success

With the exception of the successful Brabham BT 18 (3), Honda's racing cars were complex in design. The RA 271/272 (11) had a transverse 1.5-liter V12 engine.

The 3-liter V12 in the RA 300 (14) was conventionally installed. In the RA 301 (5) the same engine had its exhaust manifolds on the outside

Honda gained its first Formula 1 world championship titles in 1986 and 1987, with Williams. Its most successful period, however, was in 1988, partnering McLaren and with Ayrton Senna and Alain Prost as the drivers

tage to the motorcycle experts from Japan, familiar as they were with small cylinder units. However, this very experience led them to produce an idiosyncratic and very complex racing car. The water-cooled V12 engine with its 60° included angle was mounted transversely behind the driver. That required a central power take-off point, which effectively divided the engine into two six-cylinder units. The tiny cylinders, each with a swept volume of just under 125 cc, had four valves each. The engine's short-stroke configuration (bore x stroke 58 x 47 mm) permitted unusually high engine speeds to be reached. The Honda RA 272's engine could run up to 12,000 rpm, a remarkable figure for the time, and developed an impressive 240 bhp (177 kW). However, there was no run of vic-

For four years the McLaren Honda dominated Formula 1 racing: in 1988 and 1989 with the turbocharged 1.5-liter six-cylinder engine, then in 1990 and 1991 with the naturally aspirated 3.5-liter V10. Prost took the world champion's title once, Senna three times, and Honda scored five constructors' world championship titles.

HONDA IN FORMULA 1

American driver Ritchie Ginther (right) won the 1965 Mexican Grand Prix at the wheel of a Honda with 1.5-liter twelve-cylinder engine

tories. The reward for this apprenticeship in Formula 1 was a victory for Ritchie Ginther in the Mexico Grand Prix of 1965, the last Grand Prix in which these 1.5 liter engines were allowed.

Nobuhiko Kawamoto was already working hard on an engine for the new three-liter formula, due for introduction in 1966. The result was the RA 301 E, another V12, but this time mounted longitudinally in the chassis in the conventional manner. Once again, the power plant – with an included angle of 90° – had a central power take-off point, dividing it into two six-cylinder units and entailing an increase in size and weight. This complex construction made the Honda the heaviest Formula 1 racing car of its time and, even with World Champion John Surtees at the wheel, it never came in higher than third place.

In attempting to build a lighter car, the engineers at Honda became trapped in the new technical doctrine that in future only air-cooled engines should be used. For the 1967 season they built the RA 302. This car had a longitudinally mounted V8 at the rear. The cylinders (bore x stroke 88.0 x 61.4 mm), with an included angle of 120 degrees, were cooled solely by the airstream entering through air scoops. This alternative Formula 1 engine was indeed almost 100 kilograms lighter, but with an output of 430 bhp (316 kW) at 9,500 rpm from its eight cylinders, it was never able to match the twelve-cylinder, and offered no chance of success. Jo Schlesser's fatal accident brought both the car's career and Honda's participation in Formula 1 to an end for some considerable time.

Honda's more recent involvement in motor racing began in the same way as before – with a power unit for Formula 2. In 1979, Nobuhiko Kawamoto and his team of engineers designed the two-liter V6 engine within the space of a few weeks, working feverishly in a hotel at the foot of Japan's holy mountain, Mount Fujiyama. The RA 260 E was a naturally aspirated engine but the included angle of 60° between the cylinders and the rest of its architecture matched the subsequent turbocharged versions. Once again, it was a short-stroke design (bore x stroke 90 x 52.3 mm). Its output was superior to its European rivals, with a brake horsepower of 310 bhp at 10,500 revs. Nigel Mansell made his mark with a second place at Hockenheim in a Ralt-Honda before moving on to greater things.

On its way to Formula 1, this engine had to overcome competition from a rival within the company. The engineers were also experimenting at that time with a much more radical solution to the power question: a 1.5-liter V10 engine with a significantly higher engine speed and a lower boost pressure that supposedly gave more power and a better torque characteristic. The battle between the two designs was won by the simpler engine, a decision typical of Nobuhiko Kawamoto's pragmatic approach.

HONDA IN FORMULA 1

In 1964 the Honda RA 271/272 with V12 1.5-liter transverse engine was an attempt to revolutionize Formula 1 racing-car design. In 1965, at the end of its career it scored a win in the Mexican Grand Prix, driven by Ritchie Ginther

In 1983, the stroke of the two-liter six cylinder engine was reduced even more (bore x stroke 90 x 39.2 mm) to produce a 1.5-liter version, with forced aspiration by two turbochargers. No less than 600 bhp was the engineering department's claim. The Williams world champion team was the first to use the Honda engine, but champion Keke Rosberg took points with it only once in 1983. A fifth place at Kyalami (South Africa) was the best that the team could do.

The path to the top remained a difficult one. The 1984 season at least saw Rosberg's first victory for Williams in Dallas (USA). In 1985 Williams had Keke Rosberg and ex-world champion Nelson Piquet under contract, and things started to look up: two wins for Rosberg, two for Piquet. In the following season, Piquet had the support of the young Nigel Mansell. The overall results for 1986 were even more encouraging for Honda: four wins for Piquet and five for Mansell, who only

In 1966, when three-liter engines were permitted in Formula 1, Honda adopted a conventional layout for its V12 (above right)

The most successful Formula 2 racing car in the first few years was the Brabham-Honda BT 18, with 11 successive victories in 1966 (right)

The Honda RA 301 also won only a single Grand Prix: John Surtees took it to victory in Monza, Italy in 1967

Driving the Williams Honda FW 09, Keke Rosberg won the US Grand Prix in 1984

The Spirit 201C of 1983 was the first recent Formula 1 car to be powered by the Honda turbocharged six-cylinder engine

At the wheel of the Williams Honda FW 11B, Nelson Piquet carried off his third world championship title, and Honda secured the constructors' title for the second time

HONDA IN FORMULA 1

lost the World Championship battle to Alain Prost driving a McLaren-TAG in the last race because of a flat tire. However, Williams-Honda won the constructors' title.

In 1987, Piquet and Mansell again drove for Williams. Honda engines were also being used by a second team, Lotus, where the up-and-coming star Ayrton Senna and the Japanese driver Nakajima were on the payroll. The small six-cylinder engine had been extensively redesigned internally. The dimensions of the cylinders were not as extreme now (bore x stroke 79 x 50.8 mm) but its power was now measured in four figures: 1010 bhp (742 kW) at 12,000 rpm and a boost pressure of four bar. Torque had gone up to a massive 664 newton-meters at 9,700 rpm. With that amount of power available, Honda engines in Williams and Lotus won no fewer than 25 places on the podium, including eleven victories. Nelson Piquet won the drivers' championship for the third time and his team, Williams-Honda, once again took the constructors' title.

In 1988 there was a decisive change in the rules: the power of the turbos was reined back by limiting boost pressure to 2.5 bar. This still left the Honda engine with 685 bhp (504 kW) at 12,500 rpm. The torque curve was now significantly flatter, with a peak of 424 newton-meters at 9,700 rpm. It was with these "smooth" Honda engines that McLaren and Lotus entered the season. Alain

Prost and Ayrton Senna dominated the scene for McLaren. Prost took seven first places and Ayrton Senna eight; McLaren won the Constructors' Championship with the unprecedented total of 199 points.

In 1989 the turbo era was drawing slowly to a close. The turbocharged 1.5-liter engines, now in their last season, were up against a new generation of naturally aspirated engines with an increased engine-size limit of 3.5 liters. Honda was well prepared for the changeover. The turbocharged units were revised one final time and there were now two versions to choose from, depending on the conditions: the XE 2 for lower fuel consumption and the XE 3 for higher power at the top of the range. In addition, there was a race-ready V10 with an included angle of 72 degrees between the cylinders. Since the power of this large engine had to come from increased engine speed, the stroke was kept as short as possible (bore x stroke 91 x 53.7 mm). This enabled the 3.5-liter ten-cylinder unit to approach the figures for the small turbocharged V6, with just under 700 bhp at an engine speed significantly higher than 12,500 rpm. The engineers at Honda and McLaren decided to rely on the turbocharged units just one more time in 1989. At the end of the season, which was dominated by McLaren, Alain Prost was champion, just ahead of Ayrton Senna.

In 1990, turbocharged engines were finally

banned. The ten-cylinder engine built by Honda for McLaren, designated the RA 110, was already in its second development stage. It was designed specifically for high engine speeds (bore x stroke 93 x 51.5 mm) - the limit being above 14,000 rpm – and its power output exceeded the 700 bhp mark. Senna was now driving for the McLaren team, together with Gerhard Berger, but his toughest competitor in this season was once more Alain Prost, who was now under contract to Ferrari and put considerable pressure on the ten-cylinder Hondas with the twelve-cylinder unit traditionally fielded by Maranello. At the end of the season, though, the title was indisputably Senna's, with six wins, and the constructors' title went to McLaren for the third time in succession.

For the 1991 season, McLaren-Honda had a twelve-cylinder engine which was almost twice as powerful as its predecessor in the late sixties. In top form, this power plant with its very compact cylinder dimensions (first version RA 121: bore x stroke 86.5 x 49.6 mm; second version RA 122: 88 x 47.9 mm) delivered 816 bhp (600 kW) at 14,400 rpm and had a torque output of 405 Nm at 11,800 rpm. Senna won seven races with this engine and his championship title considerably improved McLaren's record. The team won the Constructors' Trophy for the fifth time with Honda engines and provided the champion driver for the fifth time as well. 1992 was the last season

in which McLaren used Honda engines. Two wins for Senna and two for Berger were a relatively poor result compared with the preceding years. The continued superiority of Williams and its Renault ten-cylinder engine led many to think that the move back to a twelve-cylinder design had been a step too far. At the end of the season, which concluded with a win for Gerhard Berger, Nobuhiko Kawamoto, now Honda's President, made the following announcement: "Formula 1 has served its purpose for Honda by enabling us to consolidate our position as a major international automotive manufacturer."

The year 2000 sees Honda once again hard at work in Formula 1 racing. The British-American Racing Team's cars are powered by Honda engines of totally new design, and it is hoped to offer a genuine challenge to such rivals as McLaren-Mercedes and Ferrari in the coming seasons.

The story of Honda in the American CART Series is a story of patience as well as strength. In 1994, nobody could have hoped that by the 1998 jubilee year a car with

The engine that gained Honda the manufacturer's world championship title in 1989

HONDA IN THE AMERICAN CART SERIES

Canadian driver Paul Tracy in the Reynard-Honda was extremely successful in the CART series

Honda power would have won the CART series drivers' title for the third season in succession. Back in that first year, a turbocharged V8 engine was used. The way ahead was stony at first, but who could fail to be impressed, in this engine's fifth year, not only by the triple victory but also by the sheer speed at which Honda has risen to be the supplier of horsepower to the CART scene. Naturally enough, Honda Performance Development (HPD) in Santa Clarita, California,

was prepared to pay the penalty for initial mistakes in the first season. Be that as it may, failing to qualify for the celebrated Indianapolis 500-mile race in 1994 was too much to endure. "That was a shock we don't care to look back on!" admits HPD Vice-President Michihiro Asaka.

At the prestigious Indy 500 of all places, Bobby Rahal and his team colleague Mike Groff were too slow. The first-generation V8,

182

code-named HRX, had a steel engine block and was therefore too heavy. Both power output and reliability were poor at first. On that fateful day, May 29, 1994, there was indeed a Lola-Honda to be admired in Indianapolis – but only on display by the Rahal/Hogan team in the foyer of a hotel.

To uphold his responsibility to the sponsors, team manager and driver Rahal deserted the Honda cause for one weekend and bought two of the previous year's Penske-Ilmor cars. In the actual race Rahal came in third, a situation which was even more embarrassing to Honda.

This was not to remain the American's best placing of the 1994 season. Less than two months after Indianapolis, Rahal took second place in the Lola-Honda in the City of Toronto event. This was the first sign of a breakthrough in a season which – not surprisingly with a totally new engine – was notable for its many problems. This first step up onto the winners' podium was a sign that much more was to be expected from the Honda engine. Not even Porsche or Ilmor had secured one of the first three places in their initial season. Rahal ended up that year with 59 points in the CART rankings – a most respectable tenth place.

Honda changed its strategy in 1995. To avoid too much notice being taken when a triple CART champion failed to make it into the points, young drivers in less well-known teams were to help develop the engine instead of popular driver Rahal. The choice of team fell on Tasman Motorsports, with IndyCar rookie Andre Ribeiro and also Scott Goodyear, who in fact only drove three races. During the season, Comptech Racing also joined the Honda family with its American driver Parker Johnstone.

On its second attempt at Indianapolis Honda well and truly made up for the previous year's debacle, with a second-generation Type HRH engine. Oval specialist Scott Goodyear put up the third-fastest lap speed in qualification and was therefore on the front row of the grid for the actual race. He drove a total of 42 laps. Had it not been for a time penalty incurred in the final phase of the race, when he overtook the pace car too early after a restart, he might have caused the ultimate sensation. As it was, victory went to the later champion, Jacques Villeneuve.

The Californian driver Jimmy Vasser was regarded as an "oval specialist". Cart champion in 1996, he won several 500-mile races including the last one of the 1998 season in Fontana

The second CART appearance on a big oval track in the 1995 season was the Michigan 500-mile race, and with Parker Johnstone at the wheel it was a confirmation of the upward trend. A talented pianist as well, Johnstone needed every scrap of his keyboard technique to reach pole position. Three weeks later it was Ribeiro's great day, with a win on the one-mile oval in New Hampshire.

In the following week Honda took full-page ads in many American newspapers to celebrate its first IndyCar victory. Under a picture of the colorful Tasman car, the guiding principle of company founder Soichiro Honda was displayed in big letters: "If at first you don't succeed, try, try again".

When he was a racing driver himself, Honda had learned the importance of patience and hard work for success. The company's founder had always maintained that Honda should demonstrate its capabilities by facing up to competition in motor sport. As in Formula 1 already, this was seen as a means of encouraging and motivating the company's best engineers.

And now history was repeating itself: it was not until its second season (1984) that Honda pulled off its first success in Formula 1, with Keke Rosberg in Dallas. Admittedly, it took two years more before a team using a Honda engine was able to secure the coveted constructors' title.

Six constructors' and five drivers' championships between 1986 and 1991 naturally aroused great expectations in the CART series. CART President Andrew Craig comments: "At first there was a lot of doubt as to whether Honda could upset the competition in this series." Fearing the Japanese company's immense technological experience, the CART organizing body imposed tougher overall technical conditions on the entrants, clearly hoping to avoid expensive development projects involving five valves per cylinder or even oval pistons and pneumatic valve gear.

Despite such limitations, Honda achieved its first CART title more rapidly than in the days of Formula 1, using the 2.65-liter engine with restricted boost pressure. As the supplier of horsepower to the team run by ex-racing driver Ganassi, whose interest had first been aroused by Ribeiro's win at the end of 1995, Honda became the leading source of engines in the 1996 racing season.

Californian driver Jimmy Vasser reached the finishing line in every race, won five of them and clinched the title at the final race in Laguna Seca. His new team colleague Alessandro Zanardi was victorious on three occasions and gained the title "Rookie of the Year". Of the 16 races, Honda won 11, including the two 500-mile events in Michigan. The first of these, in May, went to Vasser, who demonstrated only too clearly to the opposition that the V8 engine was capable of surviving the distance despite its output of 900 horsepower. In July it was Ribeiro's turn to secure the second win of the season in Michigan. As a consequence Honda, with 271 points, was able to claim its first constructors' championship title, followed by Ford Cosworth (234) and Mercedes (218).

With the third version of the Honda Motors engine, code-named HRR, Alessandro Zanardi continued to reach for the skies in 1997. In the first three races of the new season, as in the last eight in 1996, the Italian driver started from the front row of the grid – a CART record. In Honda circles, Zanardi began to be spoken of as "I-da-ten", the name of a god from Japanese mythology who was alleged to be "faster than light".

A racing driver through and through, Zanardi lived up to his new nickname and won five races in 1997. He was among the first three on two further occasions, collected an immense number of points and finished the season as CART champion with a total of 195. Surprisingly, although Gil de Ferran and previous year's champion Jimmy Vasser also finished well up the table, Honda missed out on the coveted constructors' title by just a few points.

For the 1998 season Honda Performance Development produced a new turbocharged V8 engine. This was the HRK, lighter, more powerful and more economical than its successful forerunner. 60 engines were built in all, ten for each car. If one includes major overhauls to race engines, about 170 new and as-new engines left the HPD workshops in the course of the season. They were all assembled in accordance with the motto quoted on a large banner on the wall of the workshop: Performance + Quality = Success.

This time out Zanardi won seven races, including four in succession. He also stood on the podium on seven further occasions and scored the unbelievable total of 285 points. No other driver has dominated CART racing to such an extent in recent years. With a win at the last event of the season in Fontana, team-mate Vasser completed the Ganassi team's double success, though he ended up 116 points behind Zanardi. As in 1997, third place once again went to a driver using Honda power, the Scotsman Dario Franchitti. With 13 victories from 19 starts, this was Honda's most successful CART season, and the constructors' title a just reward for its efforts.

31 wins in the past four years of CART racing have done wonders for Honda's publicity in the USA, but as HPD Vice-President Asaka emphasizes: "Honda has a very strong sporting spirit. We want all Americans to know this!"

Alessandro Zanardi was the most successful champion "powered by Honda": he took the title in 1997 and 1998

Brazilian driver Gil de Ferran and the Walker team carried out a lot of development work for Honda

186

WHAT IT'S LIKE TO BE PROPELLED BY 900 HONDA HORSEPOWER.

How can one describe something that goes beyond what the senses can appreciate? What is the standard of comparison for the feeling of being catapulted from 50 to 125 miles an hour within four seconds? It's no use asking CART drivers what they feel. They are regularly confronted with experiences of sheer speed that would blow the ordinary driver's mind and take the breath away in the truest sense of the term. The German folk hero Baron Munchhausen claimed to have ridden a cannonball, but unfortunately his comments have not been recorded, neither can we ask the projectile itself what it feels.

The privilege of being allowed to take the wheel of champion driver Zanardi's car is bound to leave many questions unanswered. An unsatisfactory situation: but so is the fact that although I consider myself capable of driving the Reynard-Honda, I know that I cannot claim in the slightest to have it under control.

CART cars are not intended to be driven slowly. Restrained progress with the tires still cold transmits even the slightest track surface irregularities mercilessly to the driver. The front Firestones obstinately pursue every joint in the asphalt. But as the speed picks up, the wing and undertray generate more downforce, the car abandons its efforts to pursue a zig-zag course, and the driver's adrenalin count returns to a more normal level.

But to use full throttle is to send the pulse racing at least as fast as the speed of the 2.65-liter turbocharged engine. The yellow gear-shift lamp in the cockpit, by means of which the engine management electronics inform the driver that 13,500 revs have been reached, comes on so frequently that the right hand might as well stay on the wooden gear lever knob. The sequential gear shift then only needs a quick pull to select the next-higher gear. The feet don't have to be moved: gearshifts are clutchless, at full throttle. A senson on the linkage interrupts the ignition for a few thousandths of a second.

Load reversals are therefore almost unnoticed, but the thrust is quite unbelievably strong. The roar from the two narrow exhaust tailpipes tells me that almost 900 horsepower are having no problems in shifting a weight of about 1,720 pounds (including the driver). The edges of the track flash past the Reynard at the left and right: a speed tunnel in which only the professional can keep track of things visually and aurally. Engine noise? I wasn't aware of it ...

The straights on this circuit are just long enough for sixth gear to be reached. At about 155 mph, the brakes have to be applied gently. I left the last bend in third gear no more than five seconds ago. Floor the throttle and shift gears as fast as Zanardi does, and the Reynard-Honda only needs about 3.4 seconds to rocket from 50 to 125 miles an hour.

Such data, of course, are far from answering all the questions that occur to one at the wheel of the Reynard-Honda. For example: how does it feel to be lapping the oval at 230 mph, surrounded by 20 other CART cars?

187

A VISIT TO SOICHIRO HONDA

INTELLIGENT, SYMPATHETIC, FULL OF LIFE

I N OCTOBER 1962 GÜNTHER MOLTER, EDITOR-IN-CHIEF OF "MOTOR REVUE", HAD THE UNIQUE OPPORTUNITY AS THE FIRST EURO-PEAN JOURNALIST TO STUDY THE HONDA COMPANY'S ACTIVITIES ON THE SPOT IN JAPAN. HE WAS EVIDENTLY DEEPLY IMPRESSED BY THE UNPRETENTIOUS SOICHIRO HONDA, WHO WAS AT THAT TIME ENGAGED IN CONQUERING THE WORLD!

INTELLIGENT · SYMPATHETIC · FULL OF LIFE

Tokyo, October 1962

I'd been in Tokyo for ten days. I'd driven the latest Japanese models and put in a lot of work on the Honda sports car, but I hadn't heard anything about the fabled Honda Grand Prix contender. Any mention of the subject at Honda met with a wall of silence. I would have to speak to Soichiro Honda himself. When I raised the subject with the company, there was no response. I was obliged to wait, even though I didn't have much time left. I was therefore surprised to come back to my hotel one evening and find a letter saying that Soichiro Honda would meet me the following Tuesday and that I would be picked up from the hotel at 9 o'clock precisely. On the Tuesday I was collected from the hotel at 9 o'clock sharp by a black Ford Galaxie and driven out from Tokyo to Honda's Research and Development Center at the Yamato plant. The German flag was flying over the entrance to greet the first German journalist ever to visit the works: surely much more than just a polite gesture.

In the board room there was the usual greeting ceremony: I was offered hot refreshment towels and tea and sandwiches, but there was no sign of Mr. Honda. The export director was present, and said that he would also act as interpreter, since Mr. Honda spoke only Japanese.

Some time had passed when suddenly a side door opened and in stepped an energetic but kindly man of average height, with little to distinguish him in appearance from the technical people in the factory. He was wearing a white cotton jacket and the same American-style cap as the workers. It was only when, with a friendly smile, he offered me his visiting card that I realized I was face to face with Soichiro Honda, the man who had created the impressive Honda organization. In 1962, just short of 57, he was still the moving force behind the company, then the biggest manufacturer of motorcycles in the world with an output of 85,000 units per month.

Soichiro Honda was much closer to the needs of the real world than to the administrative tasks that had to be performed within his vast business. This may be why he gave his factories such an exemplary social character, ensuring as a result a happy workforce for whom the company meant as much as their own family.

First of all, he offered his employees a stake in the company by enabling them to acquire shares at a reasonable price. In addition, they could be certain that they would not be thrown out on the street if they were ill. Honda built clinics with modern equipment for his factories and included the workers' families in this provision. If a member of the family fell ill, the plant sent an ambulance from the clinic to treat them at home. Even the workers' free time was organized if they

190

wished — company-owned vacation resorts enabled them to go on vacation at reasonable prices. Sports clubs offering everything from baseball to gliding in the company's own sail-planes catered for all tastes.

Soichiro Honda was a self-made man in the truest sense of the word. He was the son of a blacksmith and ran away from high school to become a car mechanic. At the age of 27, he already owned a garage with up to 50 employees. He started to make piston rings, but this wasn't a success. During our conver-sation, he frankly admitted that this was pro-bably due to his limited technical knowledge at the time. He quickly made up his mind to attend evening classes at a technical school, catching up in this way on what he'd missed as a mechanic. During the day, he continued to work on production but simultaneously reorganized the company using the know-ledge gained from the evening classes. Suc-cess was not far away when his work was

destroyed towards the end of the war in American bombing raids.

Just as in Germany, there was a huge post-war demand for transport of all kinds. Honda saw his opportunity. He acquired small ex-Army engines previously used to drive gene-rators for communications equipment, and fitted them to bicycles. This was the starting point for the Honda motorcycle. With an initial capital equivalent to 11,000 German Marks, he set up the first Honda factory. By 1961, the company's capital had reached 100 million Marks.

In 1962 the Honda organization, with its headquarters in Tokyo, consisted of three main plants: Saitama, Hamatsu and Suzuka, with a workforce of 6,000.

This was the racing car with 8.2-liter eight-cylinder engine with which Honda set up an absolute speed record in 1936, but in which he later had a severe accident

In 1961, for the equivalent of about nine milliion US dollars, the company built the Yamato Research and Development Center in Saitama, an ultra-modern complex employing 700 engineers. Honda had transferred 30 % of his shares in the parent company to the employees. In addition, he used his own funds to establish the American Motor Co. Inc. in Los Angeles and European Honda Motor Trading GmbH in Hamburg. During my visit, Honda indicated that he would be setting up an assembly plant in Belgium for the company's 50 cc motorcycle. A technical school for automobile and motorcycle engineering was opened in Yamato, and training schools for mechanics in Yamato and Hamatsu. Honda had learnt the importance of good training, he said, from his own experience.

Honda also recognized that he had to demonstrate the quality of his motorcycles to the public and that the best place to do this was

the race track. In 1959, his two- and four-cylinder bikes appeared for the first time in World Championship events. In 1961, they captured two World Championship titles (125 and 250 cc). Honda commented: "If you build something really good, people will buy it all over the world". Honda followed this principle in the second phase of his plan: the automobile, reminding people that he had built a racing car while still a motor mechanic. He had taken an American chassis and fitted a 90 bhp aero engine from a Curtiss JN, or "Jenny" as it was known, a First World War training aircraft. Later he raced a car powered by a supercharged Ford engine, with his brother as co-driver, but they were involved in a severe crash in which both were injured.

Nevertheless, Honda retained an affinity with motor sport. Even at the age of 57, he was much happier sitting on a fast motorbike than at a desk. In this he much resembled

INTELLIGENT · SYMPATHETIC · FULL OF LIFE

Ferdinand Porsche, who in his early years as an automobile manufacturer also took part in races and was a pragmatic thinker. Again, Honda worked closely with his engineers, often providing a decisive impetus that determined the course of development. He was well aware that in Europe the Japanese were regarded as plagiarists, but pointed out that those times were long gone and that Honda was developing its own ideas.

When I steered the conversation onto the subject of the Grand Prix car, my questions seemed to be hitting the mark: he reacted enthusiastically. I now realized that the decision to take part in Grand Prix racing was a matter of great personal importance to him. Here too, he acted methodically: in Suzuka, he built a grand prix circuit. This wasn't just a test track: he wanted a Grand Prix event to be held in Japan. He already had personnel qualified to develop high-performance engines, but chassis design was a new area. He therefore bought a 2.5-liter Cooper Climax for study purposes. The first Honda sports car had just made its debut at the Tokyo Motor Show: an attractive roadster with a choice of 356 or 492 cc engines.

Honda confirmed that the Formula 1 1.5-liter engine was based on his company's racing motorcycle engines. The result was a V12 with an output of about 220 bhp at 12,000 rpm. The first Honda Grand Prix car,

the RA 271E, made its debut at the Nürburg Ring in the German Grand Prix with the American driver Ronnie Bucknum at the wheel. Of all the circuits used in those days for the championship, Honda had chosen the most difficult for its first race.

Bucknum was last off the starting grid, having had a practice lap time of 9:34.3 minutes. The fastest driver in practice was Surtees in a Ferrari, with a lap time of 8:34.4. Bucknum retired in the 12th round after an accident.

In the fall of 1962 Soichiro Honda rolled out a prototype Formula 1 car for the 1963 season

Honda entered its
RA 271 in 1964 for
various Formula 1
events.
The first of these
was on the German
Nürburg Ring, with
Ronnie Bucknum
driving

The 271 was developed into the 272E, which won its first Grand Prix race in Mexico in 1965 with Ritchie Ginther at the wheel. This was the last Formula 1 race for 1.5-liter engines.

For the 3-liter Formula 1 season in 1966, Honda created the 273E, a 90° V12 developing 400 bhp at 10,500 rpm. By 1967, this had been increased to 420 bhp at 11,500 rpm. It was with this engine that Surtees won the Italian Grand Prix in Monza. For the 1966 season, Honda, then still contracted to supply engines to Jack (now Sir Jack) Brabham, developed the power unit for the Brabham Formula 1 from the four-cylinder 1-liter engine intended for the company's roadster. In 1966, Brabham won 11 races with this engine.

At Tokyo airport on my way home, I met Soichiro Honda again. "I'm on a business trip to California!" he said without the least hint of pretentiousness, impressing me once again with his natural dignity: a self-made man who created a global enterprise and has already entered the pantheon of automotive history.

Ronnie Bucknam had no chance on his first Formula 1 outing with the new car on the Nürburg Ring – much too heavy, the car started from the back of the grid and retired on the twelfth lap after an accident

SUZUKA AND MOTEGI

THE DEPTH OF SOICHIRO HONDA'S PASSION FOR MOTOR SPORT WAS ALREADY EVIDENT IN THE EARLY NINETEEN-SIXTIES, WHEN HE BEGAN TO ENTER HIS PRODUCTS FOR INTERNATIONAL MOTORCYCLE RACES – BUT NOT FOR THIS REASON ALONE. FOR THE BENEFIT OF HIS STILL-YOUNG COMPANY HE DECIDED TO BUILD SUZUKA, A RACING CIRCUIT THINLY DISGUISED AS A PROVING GROUND. THIS WAS PROBABLY THE FIRST TIME IN AUTOMOBILE MANUFACTURING HISTORY THAT A COMPANY HAD OWNED AND OPERATED A PUBLIC MOTOR RACING CIRCUIT.

SUZUKA AND MOTEGI

Motegi is more than just a race track built to Formula 1 standards. It is a complete leisure park in a green setting situated north of Tokyo, with facilities for various kinds of motor sport

The history of the Suzuka racing circuit started early in 1961, when a company known as "Motorsport Land" was founded. The plan to build a racing circuit was put into effect without delay. Since Suzuka was officially declared to be a vehicle proving ground, the chosen site had to be within about 30 miles of the main production plant in the Hamamatsu area and about the same distance from "motown" Nagoya.

The first major motor racing event was held there on the first weekend of May 1963. Although the Japanese Grand Prix was still unable to attract the big guns of Formula 1,

100,000 spectators turned up and saw a sports-car race with international entrants. A motorcycle Grand Prix was held later the same year, with Honda itself carrying off many of the prizes.

It was not until the 1980s, when Honda's turbocharged engine was making all the running in Formula 1, that the company reached agreement with the FIA to hold a Grand Prix event in Suzuka from 1987 on.

After this thirty-year period from the inauguration of the Suzuka circuit, at a moment when the advent of Formula 1 racing had added still further to its appeal, the Honda

In addition to a high-speed oval track as used in America and a road circuit with numerous bends, there is also a kart track and a sand racing track. When no race meeting is scheduled, private drivers are also welcome to polish their skills in Motegi

It's rush hour in the Motegi pit lane even at weekends when there is no race meeting, because the Japanese have to take to an enclosed racing circuit whenever they feel the urge to drive fast

Once a year, racing cars from the American CART series roar round this banking at speeds of nearly 220 miles an hour

200

SUZUKA AND MOTEGI

management resolved that one location capable of hosting international events was not enough for a company with such a high sporting reputation as Honda. It resolved with typical determination to build a second, more modern race track. The ground was broken for the "Twin Ring Motegi" project in February 1994.

What Honda has conceived in the hilly, wooded countryside about 60 kilometers north of Tokyo is without parallel among any of the

Races are held for young drivers and professionals on the kart track, and in Motegi small children get their first taste of mobility on a miniature railroad

201

SUZUKA AND MOTEGI

This inflatable play-tower with the features of a gigantic automobile is ideal for the kids to amuse themselves

world's motor racing circuits. The first phase of the Motegi project covers a site area of about 1.16 square miles, but expansion to a total of nearly 2.5 square miles is planned. To make sure that the track is easily visible between the hills, gigantic earthworks were needed to level off much of the valley and form an arena.

The name "Twin Ring" has been chosen because there are in fact two main circuits here, and also to express the economic chal-

lenge facing Honda on its two main export markets.

The fast oval track, the "Super Speedway" is 7,920 feet long, with its curves banked at up to 32 degrees; it is the first Japanese circuit to be built in the typical style of an American "bowl" such as Indianapolis. High-powered visitors from abroad are welcome. In 1998, the Champ Cars put in an appearance. Adrian Fernandez was the surprise winner in a Reynard-Ford entered by the Tasman team. The Honda-powered teams, normally so successful, fared less well on this of all occasions. It is planned to hold the "Motegi School of Stock Car Racing" here too, and train young Japanese drivers to compete in the American NASCAR series. Chevrolet stock cars of ample power have already been purchased.

The three-mile road course is considerably longer, and built to Formula 1 standards; it is an alternative that will help to promote Honda's second-largest export market in Europe. With many corners and fairly steep uphill and downhill gradients (6 percent), this circuit has so far not achieved its international breakthrough and is currently used for national motor sport events.

Motegi has plenty of space for spectators, which is fortunate since major international events have almost always been sold out in Japan so far. For Formula 1 races in Suzuka the demand has for some years been so far in

excess of the available ticket supply that a draw has to be held to distribute the tickets fairly. Motegi has just under 1,000 seats over the pits, another 20,000 in the two VIP areas, 40,000 inside the oval and a further 80,000 in the stands at various points – with any amount of space still available for spectator seating on the banks bordering the track.

These two imposing race tracks with their pits, drivers' paddocks and all the other facilities that major motor sport events need are of course the most immediately impressive part of the new Motegi park, but not the only interesting facilities that it provides. Since we are in Japan, a kart track built to the finest international standards is an essential in view of the popularity of this sport. "Kart Land" is about 1,250 feet long, with eleven corners per lap to keep the kart drivers busy. In addition there is a figure-of-eight "North Short Course", about 1,765 yards long with

The leisure center at Motegi has a wide variety of computer games and simulations for visitors to try out their skills, and even an authentic American Cart series pit stop to admire

203

Side-by-Side is the name given to these small single-seaters powered by a Honda twin-cylinder Transalp engine located alongside the driver. They are ideal for learning how to drift a racing car or for groups of friends to organize their own race meetings

a succession of bends (14 in all). This is intended for races with Honda's small "Side-by-Side" single-seaters, which enable their young drivers to drift authentically through the corners in open-wheeled racing cars. The driver sits alongside a 75-hhp twin-cylinder engine borrowed for the purpose from the Honda Africa Twin super-enduro motorcycle. The "Multi Course" is a dynamic aspshalted area, generous in its layout, on which all kinds of couses can be marked out for testing the drivers' skills or holding competitions of maneuvering accuracy. The "Dirt Track" is in fact a combination of two natural oval bowls with very loamy soil, 110 and 440 yards long, on which the midget cars and off-road bikes made by Honda can be driven and ridden. The channel in the center of the muddy track gets steadily deeper as the race continues. Riders of enduro motorbikes can perfect their drifting skills on loose surfaces here and there is another instruction course on how to climb steep slopes on two wheels. Twin Ring Motegi not only offers plenty of opportunities for active sport, but is also dedicated to the thoroughly politically correct policy of improving the skills of perfectly

normal drivers and motorcyclists. The "Active Safety Training Park" offers many ways of doing just this: a skid pad, a twisting track with surfaces that provide a varying amount of grip, an aquaplaning track and various other sections of road on which pupils can practise panic brake applications or the avoidance of moose, elk or any other wandering animals they could conceivably encounter, and also learn how to handle other emergency situations.

Offering so many different activities is a clear indication that Motegi is more than just a motor sport race track. It's a genuine theme park or "encounter world", and the aim is not so much for it to grow gradually but for all the facilities to be available right from the start.

Those who visit Motegi, possibly only with the aim of enjoying the miracle of being able to drive as fast as they like right in the middle of Japan, will find a first-class hotel waiting for them, a restaurant with ambitions to earn a Michelin star or two and a camp site of the neat, well-planned kind that the Japanese do so well.

Behind the stands of the racing circuit is a mall with just about everything on sale that could make a racing fan's heart beat faster. Admirers of world motorcycle champion Mick Doohan, a Honda rider of course, but

also of Alessandro Zanardi, who took a Reynard with Honda engine to success in the American Champ Car series, will find their wishes catered for on this "neutral territory" just as well as Japanese fans of Michael Schumacher or Mika Häkinnen. And between the displays of souvenirs, hungry people from two different worlds can grab an appetising snack: the Japanese will probably go for sushi or noodle soup, the Americans for a burger.

Because Motegi is vast in area and Honda happens to be one of those companies that profits by carrying people around rather than expecting them to walk, the site has its own transport system. To the great surprise of the foreign visitor, this consists of extremely archaic-looking American school busses, painted in a startling yellow color that has earned the nickname "Yellow Birds". Motegi's director Koji Tozuka has the answer ready if anyone wants to know why such unusual vehicles were imported: "We wanted to live up to our international reputation, and in any cases these busses are surprisingly cheap!"

For the use of visitors to Motegi, Honda has provided a loan fleet of bicycles with auxiliary electric motors. They are part of a trial run for a planned local transportation project called "ICVS" (Intelligent Community Vehicle System), with battery recharging and exchange stations set up at various points on the Motegi site. If it is put into effect later in a big city, ICVS will include electric cars and hybrid vehicles.

One of the destinations on which all these vehicles tend to converge is the "Honda Collection Hall", the name that Honda has given to its new museum. Half a century of dynamic progress is on display here, in a permanent exhibition that not only includes all the principal racing cars and bikes that Honda built in the past fifty years, but also many of its "power products", that is to say generating sets, lawn mowers and small agricultural machines. Some of the most successful sports motorbikes from various periods, or those that were a particular sales success, are even shown among their toughest competitors. For the younger, more active visitors the Collection Hall not only has these silent witnesses of the past to interest them, but also the "Honda Fan Fun Lab" – mobile entertainment in the form of the latest virtual amusement park with everything that the computer world can offer in the form of driving and flying simulators. On some weekends Honda's robots even make a guest appearance and show us what they can do.

Twin Ring Motegi Ltd. is one of the most cost-intensive projects that Honda has ever attempted in its 50-year history. But experience tells us that race tracks live longer than new car or motorcycle models. Suzuka has proved this: after almost 40 years it is still the country's biggest rival for the new high-tech theme park in Motegi.

RESEARCH AS A GLOBAL ACTIVITY

RESEARCH AND DEVELOPMENT, OR "R & D" FOR SHORT, MAY BE AN ENGLISH TERM, BUT IT HAS BEEN PART OF THE OFFICIAL VOCABULARY IN SOICHIRO HONDA'S EMPIRE SINCE THE END OF THE NINETEEN-FIFTIES. THE URGE TO WIN RACES COMPELLED THE COMPANY TO INTEGRATE ITS R & D ACTIVITIES CLOSELY INTO ITS COMPETITION WORK. IN JULY 1960 AN INDEPENDENT COMPANY, SMALL AT FIRST, WAS SET UP FOR JUST THIS PURPOSE: HONDA R&D CO. LTD.

RESEARCH AS A GLOBAL ACTIVITY

Honda today has high-speed tracks for production and competition cars at its proving grounds in Tochigi and Takasu

R&D spent much of the time during the first year in developing itself, since the engineers needed somewhere suitable to work. This initial task was solved in record time. The R&D Center in Wako, in the north of Tokyo, was ready for them to move in by December 1961. And in accordance with Honda's practical, no-compromise policies, a proving ground was constructed at the same time, and was ready for use a year later.

On this site, 250 kilometers south of Tokyo, the Dutch racing-circuit designer John Hugenholtz, who had already drafted out the Zandvoort circuit in his home country, created a circuit in the form of a figure of eight; it was not long before it became world

famous: in 1963 a world-championship motorcycle race event was held in Suzuka (the new circuit's name) and racing car Grands Prix have been run there since 1981. How effective was the work done in Wako and Suzuka? This question was answered convincingly by the following September. In the 1962 season Honda won constructors' titles in the world motorcycle championships – in the 125, 250 and 350 cc classes!

In the years that followed, similar evidence of tangible development progress was evident: the S 500 appeared in 1963, the first version of this small roadster. In 1964 a Honda Formula 1 racing car appeared on the starting grid for the first time and took ninth

RESEARCH AS A GLOBAL ACTIVITY

place in the German Grand Prix. In 1965 the third Honda product division was established with the E 300 portable generating set. In 1967 the compact N 360 compact car was announced, and in 1969 the four-cylinder CB 750 took Honda at a rapid pace into the exotic world of the "superbike".

All this progress and the other major breakthroughs of the first twenty years took place in Wako. The necessary testing was either carried out on the racing circuit in Suzuka or simply by taking to the Japanese roads, on which traffic was far lighter than it is today. When Wako became too small for the development of motorcycles, cars and also an increasing number of Power Products, a new development center was built in Asaka, north-west of Tokyo. to deal with the motorcycles and Power Products. Like Wako, it was a purely industrial operation that undertook design and prototype construction only. Honda had so far not created a facility that combines theory and practice or the drawing board with the proving ground.

In 1977, however, such an operation did reach the planning stage. A suitable site was found in Japan's Tochigi prefecture. In the following two years an exemplary development center sprang up, complete with a proving ground that matched the highest international standards; it was officially inaugurated in April 1979. Tochigi housed design offices, extensive prototype construction facilities, all the principal experimental equip-

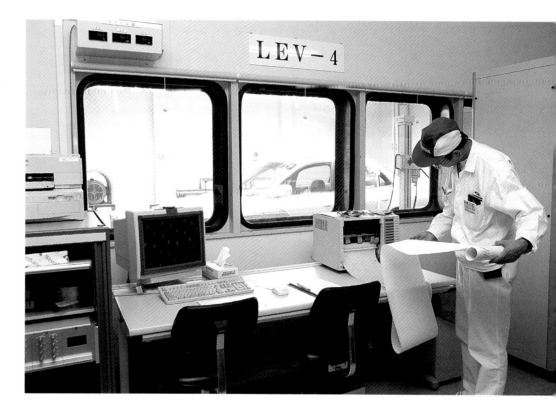

The exhaust emission laboratories, where work is in progress on cars with almost zero pollution, occupy a whole group of buildings in Tochigi

Wako also works on solving future problems, for example with this project for photo-voltaic solar cells to be produced on an industrial scale

209

Honda projects that have very little in common with the company's road vehicles: a prototype business jet aircraft which has reached the flight testing stage and the solar-powered road vehicle that won the Solar Challenge event in Australia

(On the next page)
A bicycle with auxiliary electric motor drive
Two fully mobile robots
A vehicle for the handicapped

ment and – carefully hidden away from in-
quiring eyes – the corresponding test tracks:
– a high-speed oval two and a half miles
long with curves banked at 42 degrees
– a dynamic test pad three-quarters of a mile
long and 170 feet wide
– a skid pad 330 feet in diameter
– a handling course with curve radii between
30 and 985 feet
– two absolutely straight tracks 0.75 and
1 mile long
– an experimental area with varying-grip
surfaces for testing anti lock braking, trac
tion control and vehicle dynamics systems,
together with the usual "torture tracks"

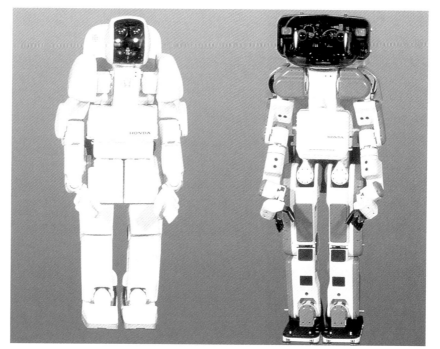

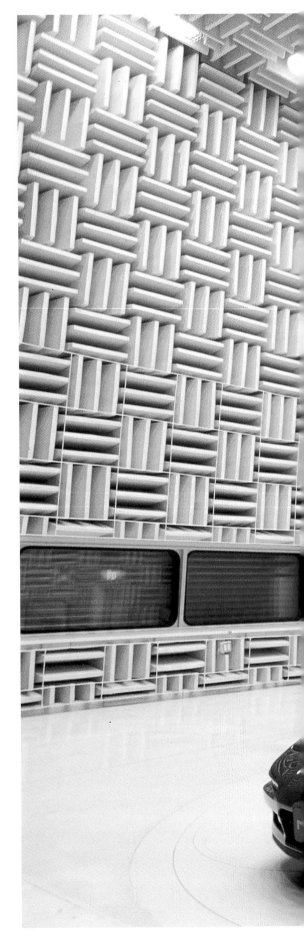

paved with blue basalt, and with wavy surfaces, cross-joints and potholes.

For enduro motorcycles and off-road vehicles there is an additional "Trail Course" including every form of rough terrain likely to be encountered on all of the five continents. And probably to make sure that the series of championship titles doesn't come to a halt, there is a one and a quarter mile moto-cross circuit as well.

An unusual sight on a motor vehicle manufacturer's proving ground are various plots of land obviously devoted to crop-growing. This is where the Power Product Division tries out its mowers or tillers.

After Tochigi had been built, the original Honda R&D operations concentrated on more specialized tasks. Asaka now only develops motorcycles, and Wako concerns itself with research, design and engine development for Formula 1. However, in recent years the research work has not been limited to product-related tasks. This is where the "Solar Racer" was developed that in 1990 won the "longest race under the sun", the World Solar Challenge held in Australia. Wako is also where the two robot projects are based, and where work is proceeding on gas turbines – and on an aircraft that could be driven by them. One could perhaps say that Wako's job is to secure the future although even Honda's management cannot always be sure what part the company will have to play in it.

Twenty years ago Honda concentrated more strongly than today on the immediate present,

213

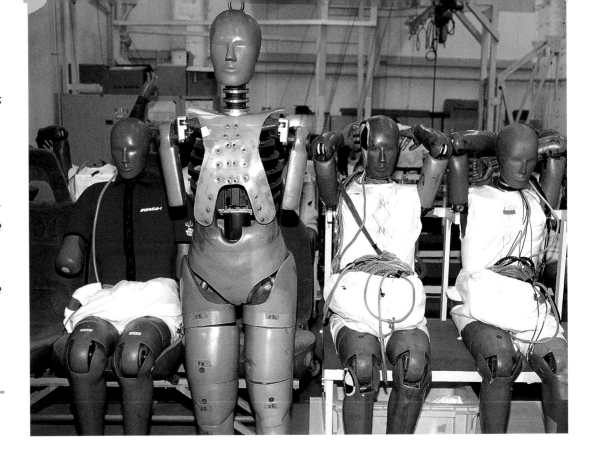

Honda not only gives its dummies the usual harsh treatment on the crash test rig, but also subjects them to systematic further development. The one in the foreground, although even the experienced observer may fail to see this, has been matched specifically to the female physiognomy

which for most of us seems to pass by at a rapid enough pace most of the time. Only a month after Tochigi was opened, Honda's R & D Center in Asaka Higashi was ready to start even more intensive work than before on the company's Power Products. This young corporate division, producing not only generating sets and agricultural machinery but also a highly profitable line of outboard motors for small boats, was able to outperform the turnover of the motorcycle division by the mid-eighties.

During this period, the activities of Honda R&D were successful although seemingly contradictory. The 1.5-liter turbocharged Formula 1 engine was built and went to the starting line for the first time in 1983. The first Formula 1 constructors' world championship was secured with Williams in 1986, and a year later the same team collected its first driver's title. Yet at the same time Honda was developing and producing its first garden tractor and also its first four-wheel-drive all-terrain vehicle, the TRX 350 4WD.

This was when Honda began to put its research and development work on a global basis. It set up Honda R&D North America in Torrance near Los Angeles in 1984. In the years which followed this American organization grew steadily, with branch offices in Detroit, Denver, North Carolina, Ohio and latterly in Canada as well. In view of its sporting activities in the USA, Honda High Performance Inc was founded, and as a means of establishing the technical truth on the spot, as it were, a further Proving Center was built in California's Mojave Desert.

Since Honda is market leader in Brazil with its motorcycles, its activities in South America are backed by R & D subsidiary operations in Sao Paulo and at the Honda plant in Manaos.

In the USA too, Honda has built some extensive proving grounds and similar test tracks. The California Proving Center has an area of 3,830 acres. Situated in the Mojave Desert, it includes a continuous track seven and a half miles long, with non-banked curves. Suspension tuning can take place on a four and a half mile long track with a large number of bends incorporated. And since the USA is such a good market for moto-cross bikes, there are suitable trial tracks here too, which can be sprayed with water to create the muddy conditions needed for authentic testing of these bikes.

The testing area in Ohio has an area of 4,500 acres and is therefore slightly larger than the one in the Mojave Desert. In Ohio too there is a continuous test track, in this case with tighter, banked curves at each end, a dynamic driving pad measuring 1,775 x 1,180 feet and two and a half miles of roughly surfaced tracks. With its own exhaust emission and crash testing rigs in the USA, Honda is able to confirm that its locally produced vehicles conform with American construction and use regulations.

Research and development work in Europe began in 1988 at Honda R&D GmbH in Offenbach, Germany. In 1992 it was joined by Honda R&D England, and there is now a technical office in Rome as well. Honda R&D is also well represented now in Japan's more immediate neighborhood, among the Asian "tiger" nations, with activities based in Singapore for the south-east Asian zone and in Bangkok for Thailand, where production facilities are now in operation.

Despite this extensive globalization, Honda's strategists know that basic progress has to take place in Japan. For this reason, planning work for yet another proving ground began in 1989 in the cool climate of the northern island of Hokkaido, where a severe winter makes the low-temperature testing possible that many markets need. The proving ground in the hills near the town of Takasu was completed in 1996 and represents an impressive alternative to the facilities in Tochigi. For suspension testing when there is no snow on the ground, a 3.85-mile circuit has been built, simulating sections of such impressive models as the north loop of the Nürburg Ring and the Spa-Francorchamps Grand Prix circuit. The design of this track is most impressive on account of its steep gradients and dramatic curves, but also contains many a surprise: for the driver new to it, every corner seems to end in an indeterminate way. There is method in this trickery: it keeps the test drivers wide awake and alert during their sessions on the track. To enhance this effect, the trees and bushes along the side of the track have been planted at completely irregular intervals.

Apart from this circuit with its violent ups and downs there is a "Country Course", nearly two miles long, which is used for road tests that resemble day-to-day driving rather more closely. Its high-speed oval track with curves banked at 35 degrees is four and a quarter miles long. For winter testing there is an entirely natural ice-covered dynamic test pad, and since this is the season of the year in which motor vehicles tend to rust, all those undergoing tests here have to go through a deep, cold salt spray.

CHRONICLE
FOR THE YEARS
1946 – 1999

CHRONICLE

The Super Cub

1946–1959

12.12.1946	Soichiro Honda founds the Honda Technical Research Institute in Hamamatsu, in the Prefecture of Shizuoka and begins to develop internal combustion engines and machine tools.
1948	Soichiro Honda converts the Honda Technical Research Institute into a corporation with a capital of one million Yen and renames it the Honda Motor Co., Ltd.
1955	Honda grows to be Japan's leading motorcycle manufacturer.
1958	The Super Cub achieves great success on the Japanese motorcycle market, making Honda the top-selling company in this business area.
1959	Honda founds the American Honda Motor Co., Inc. Among the first products from this US company are the Super Cub, Dream and Benly motorcycles.

1960–1969

1960	The Honda company's research and development work is transfered to an independent company known as the Honda R&D Co., Ltd.
1961	The Honda motorcycle racing team gains the 125 and 250 cc class titles in the Isle of Man TT races.
1962	Honda issues American Depository Receipts (ADRs) in the USA.
1963	American Honda's advertising slogan "You Meet the Nicest People on a Honda" helps to revolutionize the entire American motorcycle trade.
	Honda opens its first overseas production plant: Honda-Benelux in Belgium begins to manufacture mopeds.
	Honda issues European Depository Receipts (EDRs).
	Honda launches its first automobile and light commercial vehicle on the Japanese market.

CHRONICLE

Honda N360

1964	Honda is at the starting line for the first time in a Formula 1 race.
1965	The Honda Formula 1 racing car wins its first Grand Prix race in Mexico.
1966	Honda-powered Formula 2 cars achieve 11 successive race victories.
1967	Automobile production commences at the Suzuka plant.
1968	Honda's motorcycle sales in the USA exceed one million in this year.
1969	Canadian Honda Motor Ltd. founded in Toronto (now Honda Canada, Inc.).

1970–1979

1970	Honda begins to export its N600 cars to the USA.
	Honda Engineering Co., Ltd. founded in Japan.
1971	Honda announces the development of the CVCC (Compound Vortex Controlled Combustion) principle.
1972	American Honda Motor Co. Inc. establishes the Honda International Trading Corp.
1973	The founder and President of Honda, Soichiro Honda, and his colleague from the earliest days and Vice-President Takeo Fujisawa retire from active management of the corporation.
1974	The Civic CVCC engine is the first to comply with the US Clean Air Act of 1975 without using a catalytic converter.
	Honda becomes the first Japanese automobile manufacturer to publish consolidated accounts.
1977	In the 1977 fuel consumption test for all models conducted by the Americal environmental protection authority EPA, the Honda Civic CVCC engine is the most economical for the fourth time in succession.
1978	Founding of Honda of America Mfg., Inc. in Ohio.
1979	Motorcycle production begins at Honda of America Mfg. in Marysville, Ohio.
	Honda's proving ground in Tochigi completed.

CHRONICLE

1980–1985

1980	American Honda Finance Corp. begins its operations.
	Honda announces the construction of an automobile plant in the US state of Ohio.
1982	Honda of America Mfg. begins to produce the Accord model in Ohio.
1983	Kiyoshi Kawashima, President of Honda Motor Co., Inc., retires and begins to act as an adviser to the company. Todashi Kume assumed the title of President of Honda Motor.
	Honda returns to Formula 1 racing.
	Honda Motor Co., Inc. and the British Rover Group agree to cooperate on the design and development of a new upper midsize class automobile (the later Legend).
1984	Honda Power Equipment Mfg., Inc. begins to manufacture lawn mowers in Swepsonville, North Carolina.
	The American Honda Motor Co. sets up the American Honda Foundation.
	Honda Research of America Inc. opened in Torrance, California (originally set up in January 1975 as contact office for Honda R&D Co., Ltd.).
	Honda Motor Co., Inc. and the Rover Group agree to produce the Legend and Sterling sedans jointly.
1985	Honda de Mexico founded.
	Honda of America Mfg. begins to produce motorcycle engines at the plant in Ohio.
	Honda of America Mfg. now the fourth-largest vehicle manufacturer in the USA.

Honda Legend Coupe

CHRONICLE

Tadashi Kume

1986–1987

February	Construction work starts for a new motorcycle plant in Mexico.
March	Introduction of the Acura sales organization in the USA and start of Legend and Integra sales.
	Honda Motor Co., Inc. and the Rover Group agree that Rover should manufacture the Honda Ballade in Great Britain.
April	A second vehicle assembly line opened at the Honda of America Mfg. plant in Marysville, Ohio.
July	Production of the Civic van starts at the Marysville, Ohio plant of Honda of America Mfg.
August	Honda heads the J. D. Powers customer satisfaction charts for 1986.
September	Honda manufactures its first 1.5-liter Civic engine at the engine plant in Anna, Ohio.
	A Formula 1 car powered by a Honda engine wins the constructors' championship.
October	Honda R&D North America founded.
November	Honda of Canada Mfg. starts to produce the Accord in Alliston, Ontario.
December	Honda Motor Co., Inc. and the Rover Group agree on the joint design and development of the Concerto model.

1987

January	Honda announces an extension to its engine plant in Anna, Ohio. This investment, valued at approximately 450 million US$, is to permit the large-scale production of automobile engines and components.
February	Honda de Mexico starts production of motorcycles and vehicle components at the plant in Estado de Jalisco.
March	Acura launches the Legend Coupe.
	Honda North America, Inc. founded to coordinate Honda's activities in the USA.
	American Honda exports the first Accord sedan to Taiwan.
April	Honda launches the new Prelude, the first series-production car in the world to have four-wheel steering.

CHRONICLE

*Four times winner of the Paris-Dakar Rally –
the Honda NXR 750*

August	Acura and Honda come first and second on the customer satisfaction scale drawn up by J. D. Power.
September	Honda announces a five-step strategy aimed at making it an independent US motor vehicle manufacturer. It calls for the expansion of research and development work and of production technology, the construction of a second US automobile plant, the purchase of locally produced parts in greater volumes, expansion of the engine plant and an increase in exports of vehicles from the USA.
	The Acura Legend becomes the first Honda automobile to be offered for sale with airbags.
November	A Formula 1 car powered by a Honda engine wins the world championship. Honda's total motorcycle output in Japan passes the 50-million mark – the first manufacturer in the world to reach this figure.

1988

January	Honda of Canada Mfg. announces plans to enlarge its production capacity to 80,000 vehicles annually.
March	In the Motor Trend vote for the best imports of 1988, Honda cars take the first three places.
	Honda begins to export the Accord Coupé manufactured in the USA to Japan.
April	Honda of Canada Mfg. begins to produce Civic models at its plant in Alliston, Ontario.
	Setting up of Honda Engineering North America (originally established in May 1985 as a branch office of Honda Engineering Co., Ltd.).
	Honda's vehicle production passes the 15-million mark.
August	In the J.D. Power & Associates customer satisfaction charts, Acura comes out on top for the second time in succession; Honda is third in the overall list.
	A Formula 1 car powered by a Honda engine wins the constructors' title.
November	The construction of a research and development center in Europe is announced.
December	With more than 360,000 Accord and Civic cars produced, the Honda of America Mfg. plant in Marysville reaches its full planned output.

1989

April	Honda of America Mfg. produces its millionth vehicle, a four-door Civic sedan.
	Honda announces its intention to build a new production plant in Tochigi for the NSX sports car to be built in small numbers.
July	Honda and the Rover Group announce that they are to build a production plant in Swindon, England, alongside the Honda engine plant there. The Rover Group is to take a twenty-percent holding in Honda of the U.K. Mfg., Ltd. and Honda a similar holding in the Rover Group.
August	Acura heads the J. D. Power customer satisfaction charts for the third time, and Honda is again placed third with all its models.
	Honda of the U.K. Mfg. begins engine production in Swindon, with the emphasis on engines for the Honda Concerto and Rover 200.
September	The Rover Group (formerly the Austin Rover Group) begins to manufacture the Honda Concerto, developed jointly with Honda, at its Longbridge plant. An annual output of 40,000 units is planned for the Concerto in Great Britain.
	A Formula 1 car powered by a Honda engine wins the world championship title for the fourth time in succession.
October	Soichiro Honda is included in the Automotive Hall of Fame in Midland in the US State of Michigan.
	Honda Motor Europe, Ltd. begins operations from its head offices in London. Its purpose is the coordination of all the production, marketing, sales and service activities of Honda subsidiaries in Europe.
December	Inauguration of the new automobile production facilities of Honda of America Mfg. in East Liberty, Ohio, and start of production of Civic models.

Soichiro Honda and his wife in the Automotive Hall of Fame.

CHRONICLE

Aluminum-bodied: the Honda NSX

1990

January	Honda of Canada Mfg. plans to increase its annual production capacity from 80,000 to 100,000 units.
February	Automotive Industries magazine chooses Todashi Kume, President of the Honda Motor Company, as "Man of the Year" for 1990.
April	Honda of America Mfg. produces Accord Coupés with right-hand drive for export to Japan.
May	Founding of Honda Engineering Europe, Ltd. in Great Britain with the task of coordinating Honda's development activities in Europe.
June	American Honda transfers the head offices of its Powertrain Division from California to the US State of Georgia, not far from Atlanta.
	Honda R&D North America opens its new Experimental Center in the Californian Mojave Desert.
	Nobuhiko Kawamoto becomes President and Director General of the Honda Motor Co., Ltd.
July	In the J. D. Power customer satisfaction charts the Acura leads for the fourth time in succession.
August	Acura launches the NSX sports car, the world's first series-production car with an aluminum body.
October	American Honda plans to equip all Honda and Acura cars with driver's and front passenger's airbags by the start of the 1994 model year.
November	A Formula 1 racing car powered by a Honda engine wins the world championship title for the fifth season in succession.
December	The magazine Car and Driver includes the Honda Accord in its list of the ten best cars of the year, for the ninth time in succession.
	Soichiro Honda is presented with the FIA gold medal in Paris.

CHRONICLE

1991

January	For the third time in succession the Honda Accord is the year's top-selling car.
	The Primo dealer network operated by the Honda Motor Co. starts to sell the Jeep Cherokee and Wrangler models.
February	Honda of America Mfg. builds its millionth engine.
March	The Accord station wagon, which is built only at the Honda plant in Marysville, Ohio, is exported to Europe.
April	The Acura division launches the Vigor model, powered by an absolutely new 2.5-liter five-cylinder inline all-aluminum engine.
	The Accord station wagon, designed, developed and built in the USA, is launched on the Japanese market.
May	At the Honda of America Mfg. plant in Marysville, Ohio the five hundred thousandth vehicle leaves the assembly line – a Gold Wing Aspencade motorcycle.
	Honda Motor Co. launches Beat, a two-seater miniature convertible, in Japan.
July	Acura/Honda share fourth place in the J. D. Powers customer satisfaction charts.
August	Soichiro Honda, founder of the Honda Motor Co., Ltd. in 1948, passes away at the age of 84.
	Honda Canada, Inc. sells its millionth car since car sales began in 1973 – a Civic hatchback produced in Canada.
October	Honda introduces the new VTEC-E engine, combining its Variable Valve Control and lean-burn systems.
	Honda Motor Co. and the Rover Group sign a new declaration of intent on the development and production of various models for the future; the first of these is the new midsize car known internally as the Synchro.
	A Formula 1 car with a Honda engine wins the world championship title for the sixth season in a row.
December	Car and Driver magazine includes the Prelude S1 in its list of the ten best cars of the year.
	The Honda Civic is voted Car of the Year for 1991/92 in Japan.

CHRONICLE

Gerhard Berger in Silverstone, 1992

1992

January	The Honda Accord remains the top-selling car in the USA for the third year in succession.
	American Honda Motor Co. exports 28.205 vehicles, putting it is third place among North America's motor-vehicle manufacturers. Honda is also the leading exporter to Japan, with 14,250 units.
	Honda of America Mfg. produces its two-millionth car since production began there in 1982.
	The Honda Motor Co., Ltd. produces the twenty-millionth vehicle from its Japanese plants.
	The Honda Motor Co. announces that the number of Honda dealers who sell the Chrysler Jeep models Cherokee and Wrangler is to be raised from 100 to 300 by February 1992. By 1994 it is hoped to boost sales to 1,200 units.
	Purchases of US automotive components and materials by the Honda Motor Co., Ltd. are to be increased in volume to 4.94 billion US $ by the 1994 fiscal year (which ends on March 31, 1995). In the 1990 fiscal year Honda had purchased American automotive parts valued at 2.49 billion US $.
February	In the J. D. Power & Associates vehicle performance survey for 1992 the Acura Legend was declared to be the best three-year-old car.
	In the list issued by R. L. Polk & Company Honda leads the customer loyalty chart ahead of all other makes of car for the second time. Honda has led the loyalty ratings for imports for the past 15 years.
March	Honda R&D North America, Inc. opens its extended Research and Development Center in Ohio after an additional investment of 27 million US $ and at the same time announces that a further 25 million US $ are to be spent on another extension, to be completed in 1993.
	At its plant in Kumamoto, Honda produces the twenty-millionth Super Cub motorcycle.
	To simplify sales of cars and motorcycles in the countries of the former Soviet Union, Honda plans to open an office in Moscow.
April	Honda Europe Power Equipment S.A. is founded in Orleans, France, to centralize the manufacture, sales and marketing of powertrain equipment in Europe.

CHRONICLE

The world's most expensive production motorcycle: the Honda NR

May	Honda Motor Co., Ltd. announces the Honda NR, the first commercially available motorcycle to have oval pistons. It sells for the high price of 5.2 million Yen (39 000 US $) and is therefore Japan's most expensive motorcycle.
August	Introduction of the Honda Civic Del Sol, an innovative two-seater with a unique removable roof.
	Honda announces its first capital investment in Chinese motorcycle production, following the previous technical cooperation agreements with four local manufacturers.
September	The American Honda Education Corp. lays the foundation stone for Eagle Rock School, an "innovative high school" and vocational training center near Estes Park, Colorado.
	Honda announces its withdrawal from Formula 1 racing. Following a run of success including six championship titles in the past ten years and 15 wins in 16 races during the 1988 season, the company wishes to concentrate its efforts on fresh challenges.
October	Honda unveils a prototype solar-powered kayak named "Sun Fun". It is an experimental craft developed as part of Honda's unceasing quest for environmentally acceptable products.
November	American Honda exports the one hundred thousandth car made by the company in the USA since its vehicle export program began in 1987.
	Honda Power Equipment Mfg., Inc. starts to produce the H1011 Harmony Riding Mower at its plant in Swepsonville, North Carolina.
December	Honda Motor Co., Ltd. and Isuzu Motors Ltd. undertake a feasibility study for a Honda Marketing version of the Isuzu Rodeo in the USA.

1993

January	Honda of America Mfg., Inc. produces its two-millionth engine at the plant in Anna, Ohio, which has just been enlarged.
	Honda of America Mfg., Inc. produces its three-millionth car since 1982.
	American Honda Motor Co., Inc. considers participation in the IndyCar championships.
February	Honda Motor (China) Co., Ltd. founded in Hong Kong as a subsidiary of the Honda Motor Co. It is to be responsible for sales and service management in China.

CHRONICLE

Winner in Australia: the 'Dream' solar-powered vehicle

April

Honda Motor Co., Ltd. is Japan's largest automobile importer in the first quarter of 1993, the first time it has maintained this position for the whole three-month period. It sold 7,267 vehicles manufactured in the USA.

Under its agreement with Isuzu Motors Ltd., the Honda Motor Co., Inc. announces that it will be marketing the Jazz sports pickup, a version of the Isuzu Mu (Amigo). Honda will in turn supply a version of its Domani for sale by Isuzu in Japan.

May

In the R. L. Polk & Company customer loyalty list Honda takes first place for third time in succession, defeating all other makes of car. It is also the best import brand for the 16th time in succession.

Honda Motor Co., Ltd. establishes Honda Poland Ltd. in Warsaw to sell vehicles on the Polish market.

June

Honda Motor Co., Ltd. plans to import a new all-wheel-drive vehicle produced by Rover, to be sold with Honda badges as the "Crossroad". This vehicle is to be based on the Land Rover "Discovery" model.

July

The Acura Division introduces extensively revised versions of its Integra Sport Coupe and sports sedan.

Honda Motor Co., Ltd. plans to produce Civic sedans in Chima for the first time as part of a joint venture agreement with the Yancheng Automobile Company in the city of Guanzhou.

August

Honda R&D North America, Inc. opens a new Research and Development Center for power-train equipment at a new plant in Swepsonville, N.C.

September

Honda introduces the revised Accord model, an entirely new design.

Honda R&D North America Inc. (HRA) announces the extension of its Research and Development Center at a cost of 25 million US$, bringing total investment in the Ohio Center to 52 million US $ in two years.

Honda Motor Co., Ltd. introduces two compact cars specially designed for the Japanese market, the Ascot and the Rafaga.

October

Honda Motor extends its agreement with Isuzu Motors Ltd. The Big Horn (Trooper) is to be sold with a Honda badge and Isuzu will sell Accord sedans made in Japan under its own name.

November

The Dream solar-cell vehicle built by Honda wins the 1993 World Solar Challenge prize in Australia.

December

The Honda Automobile Division announces the Passport, its first model for the leisure-vehicle market.

CHRONICLE

*One of the world's most successful models –
the Honda Civic, here in the hatchback body style*

1994

January	Acura announces that in 1996 it will begin to sell its first model entirely designed, developed and manufactured in the USA.
February	American Honda Motor Co., Inc. breaks the ten-million US-market sales barrier for Honda/ Acura models.
	Honda Motor Co., Ltd. begins to sell the Horizon, a new leisure vehicle with all-wheel drive based on the Isuzu Big Horn (Trooper).
March	Honda Power Equipment Mfg., Inc. produces its millionth lawn mower since the production plant began operation in August 1984.
May	The twenty percent mutual participation agreed between Honda and the Rover Group expires.
June	Honda Motor Co., Ltd. announces global organizational changes which grant the four principal Honda regions – American continent, Europe/Near East/Africa, Asia/Oceania and Japan – greater independence and authority to make decisions.
July	Honda announces the adoption of a new automobile strategy for the American Continent region, with greater influence exerted by the Honda companies operating in North America within the overall global business framework.
	Acura sells the millionth vehicle it has manufactured in the USA. This record was set up in only eight years, faster than any other luxury import.
August	The ten millionth vehicle, an Accord, leaves the Sayama plant of Honda Motor Co., Ltd.
September	Honda Motor Europe Ltd. launches a Civic model to be manufactured by Honda of the U.K. Manufacturing and sold exclusively on the European market.
October	Introduction of the Odyssey, Honda's first minivan.
	Honda Cars Manufacturing (Thailand) Co., Ltd. plans to build a vehicle assembly plant near Bangkok.
December	During the year American Honda exported its hundred-thousandth car made in the USA. This earned the Honda Accord the title of number-one export model on the North American market, followed by the Honda Civic.

CHRONICLE

Honda Odyssey EX

1995

January	Honda is the first motor-vehicle manufacturer to develop a series-production gasoline engine that complies with the requirements for an ultra-low emissions vehicle (ULEV).
	Honda Motor Co., Ltd. announces that it is to build a large-scale motor sport arena known as Twin Ring Motegi not far from Tokyo. It will also offer driver training and skilled driving practise facilities.
February	Acura introduces its absolutely new TL (Touring Luxury) sedans as a sporting alternative to traditional luxury cars.
March	R. L. Polk & Co. declares the Honda Accord to be America's top-selling car to private buyers in 1994.
April	The first pupils graduate from Eagle Rock School and the Vocational Training Center sponsored by the American Honda Education Corp.
	The Acura Division of the American Honda Motor Co. announces that it is to sell the SLX luxury leisure vehicle in the USA.
May	The Governor of the US State of Ohio, George Voinovich, names Honda as "Exporter of the Year" for 1994; more than 125,000 vehicles made in Ohio were exported from the USA in that year.
	J. D. Power & Associates names Honda as the leading manufacturer in its New Car Initial Quality Study.
	J. D. Power & Associates awards its Gold Medal for Quality to Honda's Sayama plant in Japan.
June	Honda's total exports of vehicles made in the USA exceed 300,000 units.
	23 years after production started, Honda Motor Co., Ltd. manufactures the ten-millionth Honda Civic.
July	Honda introduces its Multi Matic continuously variable automatic transmission.
August	American Honda Motor Co., Inc. sells the ten-millionth car from the Honda-Division.

CHRONICLE

Premiered in October 1995:
the Honda CR-V

September

The US Environmental Protection Authority (EPA) classifies the Honda Civic in 1996 as a domestic product (made in the USA) since it has now reached a local content of 92 percent.

Honda produces its five-millionth vehicle in North America.

Honda Motor Co., Ltd. announces that Honda Vietnam Co., Ltd. will begin to manufacture motorcycles by the end of 1997.

Honda Motor Co., Ltd. announces that Honda Siel Cars India Ltd. will build a motor-vehicle plant near New Delhi. The middle of 1997 is quoted as the probable date for production to start.

October

The US environmental protection authority announces the most economical cars of 1996: there are four Honda models in the top ten.

The CR-V sports pickup with four-wheel drive is launched in Japan.

Honda passes the 30-million mark in total vehicle production, ten million of these vehicles having been manufactured in the past five years.

November

Honda de Mexico starts to manufacture vehicles for the Mexican market.

December

Automobile Magazine chooses the Honda Civic as "Car of the Year" for 1996.

The committee appointed to choose the Japanese car of the year votes for the Honda Civic.

Honda Automoveis do Brasil Ltda. announces that it is to build a motor-vehicle production plant and begin to operate it in the summer of 1998.

1996

January

The Acura Division introduces the CL model line, the first model from a luxury import brand to be designed, developed and produced in the USA.

February

Acura introduces the 3.5RL, the range-topping model of its new luxury line.

March

With 86,957 vehicles sold within a single month, Honda Motor Co. achieves the highest monthly sales figure in the company's history.

April

American Honda Motor Co. unveils the Honda EV, a four-seater electric car, to be marketed in California in the spring of 1997.

Honda Cars (Thailand) Co., Ltd. begins to sell the City sedan, a model specially designed and built for the Asian market.

May

Honda announces a speeded-up vehicle strategy for its American Continent region, with a 50-percent build-up in the production of automobile engines and automatic transmissions.

CHRONICLE

The Valkyrie motorcycle, which is built only at the Honda motorcycle plant in Marysville, Ohio, is to be exported to Japan.

June	Honda announces plans to build the Anadolu Honda Otobilcilik A. S. plant in Gebze, Turkey as a joint automobile manufacturing venture.
July	On the customer satisfaction scale for small commercial vehicles drawn up by J. D. Power & Associates, Honda takes first place.
	The millionth motorcycle, a Gold Wing Aspencade, leaves the assembly line at the Honda motorcycle plant in Marysville, Ohio.
	Honda Motor Co. sets up a joint-venture company – die Honda U.G.R. Co. Ltd. – in Japan with the task of developing recycling technologies and plant.
September	Although Honda is only at the start for the third time in the PPG IndyCar championship, it wins all three main titles in 1996 – world championship, best newcomer and best driver.
October	Honda achieves record sales in 1996 for the Honda Civic and for the Honda Division as a whole.
	The Honda Dream, a solar-powered vehicle built by the Honda Motor Co., breaks all speed and time records in the World Solar Challenge race in Australia. During the 1,866-mile race from Darwin to Adelaide, the Honda Dream achieves the record average speed of 55 miles per hour.
November	American Honda Motor Co. opens a new parts distribution center in Loudon, Tennessee at a cost of 30 million US $, to supply parts to Honda automobile, motorcycle and power-unit dealers.
	American Honda Motor Co. announced the sale, starting in the fall of 1997, of the natural gas-powered Civic GX an, which is capable of achieving exhaust emissions of only one-tenth of those currently applicable to ULEV (ultra-low emission) vehicles in California.
December	The magazine Car and Driver includes the new Honda Prelude SH and the Acura Integra in its list of the ten best cars of 1996.
	Honda Motor Co. sells a record number of cars and small commercial vehicles in Japan during 1996 – 34 percent more than in the previous year.

CHRONICLE

The 1997 Honda CART racing car

1997

January	Industry Week magazine includes the continuously variable transmission (CVT) available in the Honda Civic HX Coupé, in its list of the "25 Best Technologies of the Year".
	Honda's automobile output climbs to the record level of 779,856 units, equivalent to an increase of 15 percent.
February	Honda begins to sell the CR-V sports pickup in the USA.
March	Honda Motor Co. announces that its revised Domani sedan is the first model produced in Japan to use imported panels stamped in North America. They come from Honda's plant in Alliston, Canada.
April	Acura wins four "Best Value of The Year" prizes from Intellichoice, an independent market research company and publisher of a consumer magazine for car owners.
	Honda is the only automobile manufacturer to reach the first three every year since the J. D. Power U. K. customer satisfaction survey began in 1993.
May	American Honda Motor Co. announces that it is to build a new production plant at an investment cost of 30 million US dollars. The new Honda of South Carolina Mfg. company in Timmonsville, S.C. is to produce off-road vehicles, starting in the fall of 1998.
	Honda's EV-PLUS electric car goes on sale at four dealers in California.
	J. D. Power & Associates awards its Platinum Prize for Quality to the plant in Marysville, Ohio, and its Gold Prize for Quality to Honda's Sayama plant in Japan.
June	Presentation of 22 and 31 cc micro-four cycle engines for use in handheld power tools. These are truly all-purpose power sources that can for instance be turned in any direction and even operate reliably upside-down.
July	The OHC principle is applied to small engines so that the toughest exhaust emission limits anywhere in the world can be met.

October	Presentation of the F6C luxury cruiser, the VTR 1000 Firestorm and the FES 250 luxury scooter with four-cycle engine.
	Honda produces its 100-millionth motorized two-wheeler at the Hamamatsu plant.
November	Texan rider John Kocinski on Honda RC 45 wins the 'superbike' world championship. Michael Doohan (Honda NSR 500) is world champion for the fourth successive season in the 500-cc class. Max Biaggi wins the 250-cc world championship on an NSR 250.
December	Production of power equipment reaches the 30-million mark.
	For the first time, car production in Japan exceeds 800,000 units in a year. The CR-V Championship Male leisure vehicle is introduced.

1998

April	Introduction of the BF 130, the world's most powerful four-cycle outboard motor.
May	Presentation of the VFR 800, a motorcycle with closed-loop, three-way catalytic converter and very low exhaust emissions, the new NT 650 V Deauville midsize tourer, the new Hornet naked bike, the FES 125 Pantheon high-tech motor scooter and the new X8R-SR scooter models.
June	Introduction of the Civic Aerodeck, entirely built in Great Britain, and a completely new version of the Honda Accord.
July	Presentation of the EU series of inverter power generators, with 50 percent more compact dimensions and 50 percent lower weight than conventional generators. A special feature: the output voltage fluctuates even less than that of the public electricity supply.
October	Michael Doohan wins the 500 cc world motorcycle championship for the fifth time on Honda; Tomomi Manako is champion in the 125 cc class.
November	For the second time in succession, Alessandro Zanardi wins the CART championship for Honda.

CHRONICLE

*A step into the new millennium:
the Honda Insight*

1999

February	Introduction of the HR-V lifestyle-mobile and a new B-segment model, the Logo.
March	Worldwide market launch of the new generation of power generators using the inverter principle.
April	The Honda Motor Company's turnover of approximately 50 billion US dollars is the highest achieved in its history.
May	The Honda S 2000 is introduced to journalists.
June	Start of Honda Accord 4-door hatchback production for the European market in Swindon, England.
July	The foundation stone is laid in Swindon for the second European automobile plant.
August	Honda becomes the second-largest automobile manufacturer in Japan.
September	World launch of new motorcycle models: CBR 900 RR Fireblade, VTR 1000 SP, X 11 and XR 650 R.
	World premiere at the German Motor Show in Frankfurt of the first gasoline-fueled car in the world to consume only three liters per 100 kilometers (79 US mpg); the Honda Insight.
	Presentation of the Honda HR-V with four-door body.
October	Restructuring in Europe: Honda Motor Europe (North) and Honda Motor Europe (South) set up as new companies.
	First driving event for the media with the Honda FC-X fuel-cell car.
	The Jordan-Mugen-Honda team with driver Heinz-Harald Frentzen comes third in the Formula 1 constructors' and drivers' championships.
	Honda cars driven by Tom Kristensen and Gabriele Tarquini come third and fourth in the German Super Touring Car racing championship.
	Emilio Alzamora (125 cc) and Alex Criville (500 cc) win the world motorcycle riders' and constructors' championships for Honda in two of the three engine-size categories.
	In the American Champ Car series, currently America's most popular racing event, Juan Montoya, Dario Franchitti and Paul Tracy take the first three places and also the engine manufacturer's title for Honda at the end of the season.
	Honda announces that it will return to Formula 1 in 2000.